THE CRANBERRY CONNECTION

Second Edition

CRANBERRY COOKERY

with flavor, fact and folklore,
from memories, libraries and kitchens
of old and new friends – and strangers

compiled at
cranberrie cottage in
granville centre, nova scotia, by

Beatrice Ross Buszek

The Stephen Greene Press
Brattleboro, Vermont

First edition published in Canada, 1977

Second edition published November 1978
Second printing December 1979

Copyright © 1977, 1978 by Beatrice Ross Buszek

This book has been produced in the United States of America. It is published by The Stephen Greene Press, Brattleboro, Vermont 05301.

Library of Congress Cataloging in Publication Data

Buszek, Beatrice Ross, 1922-
The cranberry connection.

1. Cookery (Cranberries) I. Title.
TX813.C7B87   1978   641.6'4'76   78-13387
ISBN 0-8289-0337-9

*This collection of Cranberry recipes
is dedicated,
with love, to my mother,*

Irene (Spence) Ross

*and
to all the other unsung heroines
of
Nova Scotia*

ACKNOWLEDGEMENT

To all those who shared a recipe with me, and to the special few who gave generously of their time and interest as well as their recipes, many thanks.

Some recipes were taken from, or adapted from, collections compiled by the Canadian Government; from Ocean Spray Cranberries, Inc.; from Woman's Day Kitchen, and Better Homes and Gardens; from a variety of assorted newspapers & magazines. Most of the recipes were contributed by friends or relatives, or were created at Cranberrie Cottage.

The information and support from Robert A. Murray, horticulturist at the N. S. Department of Agriculture in Truro was most helpful, as was the response from the Kentville and Cape Cod Experimental Stations, and the Department of Consumer Relations for Ocean Spray Cranberries, Inc. in Massachusetts. To all the others who added to my files on the cranberry, one way or another, many thanks.

The sketches were done by Christine and Jeanie, and the photos by Dick Longmire.

Second Edition

The second edition of The Cranberry Connection includes additional recipes received from readers. I loved the many letters and comments and suggestions and recipes from women across Canada and the United States. Many, many thanks.

And thanks too, to Professor Tomkins in the Pomology Department at Cornell University, Ithaca, N.Y. for his assorted insights and comments and references.

EAT

EAT

Cookery means....the knowledge of all herbs and fruits and balms and spices, and all that is healing and sweet in the fields and groves and savory in meats. It means carefulness and inventiveness and willingness and readiness of appliances. It means the economy of your grandmothers and the science of the modern chemist; it means much testing and no wasting; it means English thoroughness and French art and Arabian hospitality.... — Ruskin.

Bonnie Brunch

Entrees

Fish and Fowl

Meat

Glazes

Grilled Goodies

Jams & Jellies

EAT

Quick Breads

Muffins

Salads

Assorted

Luncheon Salads

Molded

EAT

Potpourri

EAT

DRINK

AND BE
MERRIE

WITH

FESTIVE

CRANBERRIE

Pies

Toppings

For best results
when stringing popcorn
and cranberries, sit
in front of an old
Franklin stove.

PREFACE TO SECOND EDITION

It is nearly two years since I moved into Cranberrie Cottage where the bog adventure began. Even as with one's first child, so with THE CRANBERRY CONNECTION; despite its fledgling parent, the book took on a character of its own and rapidly outgrew its first edition.

Visitors to the Maritimes and gifts from Nova Scotians were enormously helpful in spreading the good word about year-round cranberry cookery. Many letters and cherished recipes were later received from enthused Canadian and American women—and men too—from the kitchen novice to the seasoned gourmet. Some letters were wistfully curious about the small peninsula whose Latin name means "New Scotland." For many people the book was a reminder of their roots, or of visits among the "Bluenosers," a name synonymous with Nova Scotians; a name that conjures up visions of the saucy salty spray of the North Atlantic and the fabulous fogs of Fundy.

It is now the month of May. The Hawthorn and the Mulberry trees along the fence by Cranberrie Cottage are in bloom and across the lane, along the edges and high spots of the bog, if you look closely you will see, half hidden among the leaves deep in the mossy green, wee shy pink and white blossoms with a fragrance so haunting it is never in a lifetime forgotten. It is the Mayflower—the Trailing Arbutus—the flower of the Province of Nova Scotia and, yet another link with New England, it is the State Flower of Massachusetts too.

Some oldtimers in the area told me that the Indians taught the early settlers to reckon the best planting season by the advent of these earliest blossoms. So the buds of the Hawthorn, Mulberry and Mayflower are sure signs that the cranberry vines, although as yet unseen, are already sprouting new uprights in all directions, preparing for the blossoms and then the berries that will fatten and redden for the ruby harvest in October.

And so the bog adventure goes on. It should continue to go on as nature provides her bounty and as long as there are those people who are intrigued as I am intrigued by the blending of new ideas with treasured memories. But perhaps those for whom the cranberry caper will continue to be the greatest challenge and delight are the many culinary artists who continue to be inspired by the variety of new cranberry concoctions, linked with nostalgia, as found throughout THE CRANBERRY CONNECTION.

Cranberrie Cottage
May 10, 1978

INTRODUCTION

Someone asked me where I got the idea for a cranberry cookbook. It was a simple question but with not so simple an answer. I thought on the many events of the past year, and it occurred to me to put them together; to write the story of the bog adventure before getting into the berries.

As the tale unfolded the pages soon outnumbered the recipes. It would fill a second book to recount the many beginnings, diversions and intrigues of the cranberry caper; for example, after many years away, I returned to the land of my childhood and bought a little old house overlooking a deserted cranberry bog in the Annapolis Valley of Nova Scotia. What a wonderful spot! I shall always remember the first time I stood in the yard and looked all around me.

The house sits on a knoll alongside the post road just off the main highway. The nearest neighbor is an old Baptist Church and the early morning sun rising out of the mist shines through its windows, blessing the little house with its golden rays. The North Mountain rises abruptly in front protecting the valley from the fogs of Fundy. At the back, sparkling through the oaks and maples, is a once tidal river with an everchanging mood and face, as if never again quite sure who it is but with a million memories of the days of the wooden ships and the blowing sails. Along its banks, Troop's cows wend their way each day as if guided by some inner timepiece; behind the river the South Mountain gently curves along the horizon.

Last June I moved into the house and in October came the crimson harvest. I fired up the old kitchen range and began to cook and experiment, beginning with a spiced version of cranberry sauce. The cookbooks were not much help as, like myself, most cookbook editors had thought of the cranberry mainly in terms of turkey, but here and there I found creative and tested ideas using this inexpensive native fruit with its unique brisk autumn flavour and high Vitamin C content.

My mother was amused at the sudden cranberry craze but she was also astounded. Some Nova Scotian mothers still believe that a daughter who goes off to the "States" is automatically neither interested in nor skilled in kitchen happenings. She thought it was silly to bother with "those sour berries" when "everyone knows they are only good to make sauce." Mother is now a cranberry convert.

And there were things that only obscurely relate to the origins of the cookbook, like the day I climbed into the attic of the little house and found a bundle of old diaries. I read and read; the diaries upset me. I began to feel very close to the woman who wrote them. Her life seemed a yearly repeat of the same routine and the only diversions from her duties being Church and cranberries. As I think on it now, I wonder if she had any choice about Church or cranberries either. I was glad when I read that she liked to walk across the road in the wet early morning July grass to find the spots where the cranberry blossoms were most plentiful and pinkest, and that she would pick a sprig and put it in a jar on the windowsill in the kitchen.

The cranberry quest opened many old and new doors to the past, revealing such things as the many links between the "Boston States" and Nova Scotia, and of the early planters from New England prior to the coming of the loyalists, who developed this section of the province, sowing seeds of their culture wherever they settled. And I read of old Cape Cod, and how the cranberry was first cultivated there and later in 1860 in Nova Scotia, marking its first cultivation in Canada. Now, 117 years later, I am in the midst of another cranberry adventure.

In November I spent a couple hours in the botany laboratory at Acadia University, where, among other varieties, the large American Cranberry *(Vaccinium macrocarpon)* and the wild foxberry *(V. vitis-idaea)* are well researched. My mind wandered as I recrossed the campus, pondering on all that I had learned about the cranberry — its colorful past and even brighter future. In the midst of my wanderings, a cranberry cookbook took shape in my head and I could imagine the pages with bits of fact and folklore as could be fitted between the recipes. Later, I asked the assistant to check out a library book for me. He looked surprised and I said, "I'm writing a cranberry cookbook." There was an instant of unguarded disbelief on his face, and then he grinned and said, "And I suppose you'll call it, THE CRANBERRY CONNECTION." And—I did.

The long winter weekends at Cranberrie Cottage were spent sorting, testing, creating and printing recipes. The country smell of the wood stove in the kitchen and the apple wood flames in the Franklin filled the house and me with a feeling of warmth and excitement. It was uncanny how accurately my mood, or liking for the recipe, or time of day or night, was reflected in the hand-printed pages. Later I could easily spot those recipes printed over the holiday season when I was snowbound for eight days, or those printed during a long dreary rainy spell. Many recipes were discarded, keeping those I liked best and hoped would win over cranberry skeptics. And I smiled to myself when I thought of those who might not agree with my judgement about a particular recipe, and who might then start to see RED. I would tell them, "This is the beginning of your very own cranberry caper."

The lack of traditional cookbook order in THE CRANBERRY CONNECTION is not by chance. The design, or lack of same, is a sort of outpouring of recipes, fact and folklore. My mother has an old scribbler with the same peculiar kind of order, and in it, either written, printed or pasted, are the recipes of her life. I always marvel how she can find a certain recipe, almost as if she knows where each one fits in the life and thickness of the scribbler. Her system introduced me to concoctions I would never have known had I relied only on an index or if, for example, all the pies and only pies were arranged together. I compromised in the cranberry cookbook, providing a table of contents to balance the outpouring of recipes.

The cookbook was nearly finished when spring finally found the valley. There were by now several files of correspondence, research and literature on the cranberry and I had reached the point of jacket design for the book. It was then that I made another decision — a more difficult decision than earlier ones, and again I smiled, knowing there were those who would attribute this hesitation to my roots in the Maritimes. I decided to borrow the money, to find a printer, and to publish the cookbook myself. After nearly a year with THE CRANBERRY CONNECTION, it seemed part of the family. I welcomed the challenge to shape its future and watch it mature.

In the days of the wooden ships, and especially on the whaling ships, when men were at sea for months without fresh provisions, barrels of cranberries were common fare. The men would receive a handful of red berries daily to offset scurvy. In those days there was little scientific knowledge of the high Vitamin C content of the berries.

CHRISTMAS SALAD
1½ c. sugar — 1 c. water — 4 c. cranberries
1½ t. gelatin — ¼ c. cold water — 1 t. lemon juice
¾ c. chopped walnuts — 1 c. diced celery

Boil sugar with 1c. water for 5 minutes. Add cranberries and cook slowly without stirring until they burst. Soften gelatin in cold water and dissolve in hot sauce. Add lemon juice and cool. When almost thickened fold in nuts and celery; transfer to mold and chill till firm. Serve with cream cheese and sour cream blended together.

CAPTAIN TOM'S CHICKEN STEW

2 chickens, cut-up. (about 2 lbs. each)
salt, pepper, flour — Juice of 1 lemon
¼ c. each butter and corn oil — ¼ c. flour
1 can jellied cranberry sauce
1 can stewed tomatoes
1 can (6 oz) sliced, undrained mushrooms

Sprinkle chicken with salt and pepper
and coat with flour, shaking off excess.
In large skillet heat butter and oil.
Brown chicken on all sides. Drain excess
fat. Add cranberry sauce, tomatoes
and lemon juice. Cover and simmer
about 1 hour.
Remove chicken to a platter and keep
warm.
Mix mushroom liquid and flour until smooth.
Add mushrooms. Stir into pan juices
until sauce thickens. Season to taste
with salt & pepper and spoon over
chicken.   Serves 6.

ST. GEORGE'S STREET, ANNAPOLIS. From the Fort Grounds.

3

During and after the American Revolution many people from the colonies, who were loyal to the crown, were forced to leave America. Over 20,000 came to Nova Scotia. What a shocking experience to come to an undeveloped country, only 25 years after the founding of Halifax. What a welcome sight it must have been to find the familiar cranberry.

LOYALIST COOKIES

½ c. butter — ¾ c. brown sugar
¼ c. milk — 1 c. white sugar — 1 egg
2 T. orange juice — 3 c. flour* — ½ t. salt*
1 t. baking powder* — ¼ t. baking soda*
1 c. chopped nuts — 2½ c. CRANBERRIES

Preheat oven to 375°. Cream butter and sugars together. Beat in milk, orange juice and egg. Sift together the four dry ingredients*. Combine with the creamed mixture. Blend well. Stir in chopped nuts and coarsely chopped CRANBERRIES. Drop by tsp. on greased cookie sheet. Bake 10 to 15 mins.
Makes about 12 dozen tea size cookies.

Variation: To bake as bar cookies, spread batter on well-greased pan - 11 x 15 x 1. Bake at 350° for 45 mins. or until golden brown. For sugary crust, sprinkle with granulated sugar.
Makes 48 1x2-inch bars.
These COOKIES freeze well.

CRANBERRY ORANGE MUFFINS

1¾ cups sifted flour - 2 Tablespoons Sugar
2½ teaspoons baking powder - ¾ teaspoon salt
1 well beaten egg - ¾ cup milk - ¼ c. sugar
⅓ cup cooking oil - 4 T. butter (margarine)
⅓ cup homemade CRANBERRY-ORANGE RELISH.

Sift together flour, 2T. sugar, baking powder
and salt. Mix well. Combine egg, milk
and oil. Add to dry mix and stir until
moistened. Spoon half the batter into
12 2½ inch greased muffin cups. Top
each with 1 teaspoon Cranberry-Orange Relish.
Then fill with batter mix. Bake 25 minutes
at 400°. While still warm, dip tops in
melted butter, then in the ¼ c. sugar.

Homemade CRANBERRY- ORANGE RELISH is
easy to make. Keep some in the 'frig
for unexpected guests - or combine for
special parties.

Remember - Put 4 cups berries and
2 oranges, quartered, through grinder.
Stir in 1½ cups sugar. Chill or freeze.

Statistics Canada lists cranberries
in pounds. A barrel of berries
weighs 100 lbs. In the United
States, most crop reporting services
list cranberry production by barrels.
1976 in USA = 2,257,000 bbl. or 225,700,000. lbs.

Freezing Cranberries.

Freeze cranberries and use all seasons.
Put fresh berries in plastic bag or box and
then into the freezer.   Later, just pour
out as many as you need. Rinse - drain,
and cook or chop. It is not necessary
to thaw berries.

The Pequot Indians of Cape Cod and
the Leni- Lenape tribes of New Jersey
called the cranberry ibimi , meaning "bitter berry."

CRANBERRY WALDORF

Combine ground cranberries
(2 cups) with 3 cups small
marshmallows and ¾ c. sugar.
Cover and chill overnight.

Add :
 2 cups diced unpared apples
 ½ " seedless green grapes
 ½ " broken walnuts
 ¼ t. salt
Then Fold in: 1 cup whipped cream.
Chill. Serve in large bowl or individual
lettuce cups. Garnish with green
grape clusters and fresh cranberries.
Makes 8 to 10 servings.

6

CRANBERRY TEASER

2 c. cranberry cocktail ⌣ 1 T. sugar
4 thin slices lemon ⌣ 2 c. orange juice
¼ t. each cinnamon and nutmeg

Mix well. Simmer over low heat
about 10 mins. Remove lemon slices.
Serve hot: Garnish with orange.
Serve cold: Simmer lemon, sugar,
    spices with 1 c. cranberry
    juice. Add rest of juices.
    Chill.

The first record of
cranberry cultivation
was in the hamlet of
Dennis, on Cape Cod.
That was in the
year 1816.

REFRIGERATED CRANBERRY CHUTNEY

4 c. cranberries	1 c. brown sugar
2 oranges	½ t. ginger
1 lemon	2 T. candied ginger
2 apples	2 T. grated onion
1 c. raisins	6 T. green pepper

Core apple and put fruit through
chopper. Add remaining ingredients.
Mix well. Cover and store in cool
spot or refrigerate. Makes 5 pints.

FRUIT STREUSEL PIE

Combine:

    2 cups CRANBERRIES

    2 " sliced pared apples

    1½ " sugar

    3 T. quick-cooking tapioca

    1 t. grated orange peel

Mix well.

Spoon into pastry shell.

Combine:

    1 cup sifted flour

    ⅓ " brown sugar

    ⅓ " grated sharp cheese

    ¼ " butter, softened

Crumble over pie.

Bake 30 minutes (400°).

Cover with foil and bake 15 mins. more

The temperate climate of Nova Scotia, warm days and cool nights, made it a natural setting for cranberry cultivation. The Nova Scotia fruit is considered among the best in No. America.

CRANBERRY CUTOUTS

Jellied cranberry sauce is an easy garnish. Chill the can of sauce. Slice ½ inch thick. Use a variety of cookie cutters to make unique decorative cutouts for salads, sandwiches, desserts, and main dishes. ▢ ○ ◇ ♡ ▭

CORNELL CRANBERRY PUDDING (steamed)

1 c. flour — 1 t. baking powder — 1 t. salt
1/3 c. br. sugar — 1/2 c. bread crumbs — 1 egg
2/3 c. suet, chopped — 1 cup CRANBERRIES
— 1/3 cup water —
Mix above ingredients. Turn into greased
mold. Steam 2 hours. Serve with
CRANBERRY FOAMY SAUCE.
↑

1/2 c. sugar — 1/2 c. butter
1 egg, beaten — 1/2 t. vanilla
2 t. cranberry juice

The first cranberry cultivation in
Canada was in Nova Scotia, in
1860. By 1874, the berries were
being exported as far away as
London, England.

CRANBERRY-APPLE DORIS (MOLD)

2 c. cranberries — 2 1/2 c. apple juice
2 env. gelatin — 3/4 c. sugar - Dash salt
Combine berries and 1 c. juice. Bring to
boil and cook gently about 5 mins. Soak
gelatin in 1/2 c. juice for 5 mins. Press
cranberries through a sieve, add rest of
apple juice and sugar and salt. Heat
just to boiling point.
Add soaked gelatin and stir until dissolved.
Pour into 4-cup mold or individual molds.
Chill until firm. Unmold on lettuce and
garnish with softened cream cheese.

9

The Cranberry Growers
Association started in
Massachusetts in 1864.
This marked the beginning
of the cranberry culture
as we know it today.
Eventually the cranberry
became an American Tradition

CRANBERRY ICE CREAM PIE

Combine 1½ cups gingersnap crumbs and
4 T. melted butter. Press firmly into 9-inch
buttered pie plate. Bake 6-8 mins. at 375°.
Cool. Fill with Vanilla Ice Cream (1 quart).
Top with 1 can cranberry sauce.
Freeze 6 hours

CRANBERRY-PEAR PIE

3 cups cranberries   1 cup water
1½ " sugar   ¼ " cornstarch
¼ teaspoon Cinnamon
2 cups pared, sliced pears (3)

Combine CRANBERRIES and water. Bring
to boil. Simmer 3 mins. Mix sugar,
cornstarch & cinnamon. Add to hot
CRANBERRIES; cook quickly, stir constantly.
Remove from heat when thickened. Gently
stir in pears.
Turn into pastry shell. Add lattice top.
Seal and crimp. Bake 35-40 mins. - 400° oven.

10

BOG FOG

Combine ½ c. orange juice, ¼ c. vodka and ½ c. cranberry juice cocktail. Stir briskly. Serve over ice in tall glasses.

It's the **SCOOP** of the season! Cranberries are now available year-round.

CRANBERRY CORNBREAD

1½ c. flour	¼ c. soft butter
3 t. baking powder	2 eggs
1 t. salt	1 c. canned pumpkin
½ c. sugar	½ c. milk
1 c. yellow cornmeal	1 c. cranberries
½ c. chopped walnuts	

Preheat oven to 350°. Grease a loaf pan - 9 x 5 x 2¾ inch.
Sift flour with baking powder and salt. In large bowl, beat sugar, butter and eggs. With wooden spoon stir in flour mixture, stirring until combined. Gently stir in nuts and cranberries and remainder. Bake 1 hour or until tester comes out clear. Cool on rack for 10 mins. before removing from pan. Serve warm or cold.

SPICY CRANBERRY CUPCAKES

½ c. shortening — 1 c. brown sugar
1½ c. all-purpose flour — 2 eggs
1 t. each cinnamon and nutmeg
½ t. salt — ½ teaspoon baking soda
½ c. dairy sour cream - ½ c. walnuts
½ c. jellied cranberry sauce
Golden Butter Frosting

Cream shortening and sugar. Add eggs
and beat well. Sift together dry items
and add to creamed mixture alternately
with sour cream and cranberry. Beat
till smooth. Stir in chopped nuts. Fill
paper cups half full. Bake at 350° for
20-25 minutes. Cool.

Frosting: In small bowl, mix ½ c. butter
with 1 egg yolk, 2 T. milk or buttermilk,
½ t. vanilla, and 3 c. sifted Confectioners
sugar. Blend well. Beat at medium speed
for 3 minutes. If too soft, add more
sugar. Garnish cupcakes with cranberry
cutouts. Add Cranberry juice for color.

The cranberry was used as a symbol
of peace by the chief of the
Delaware Indians. The name of
this chief was Pakimintzen, and
with time his name passed into
popular usage. PAKIMINTZEN means
cranberry eater.

PORK CHOPS with CRANBERRY

8 pork chops   3 T. sugar
1 t. cinnamon — ¼ t. nutmeg — ¼ t. cloves
½ c. port wine — 1 c. cranberry sauce

Brown chops very well on both sides.
Remove to large shallow baking dish.
Combine remaining ingredients,
except sauce, and heat until sugar
dissolves. Add sauce and heat.
Pour over chops and cover dish
with foil. Bake at 350° about
45 minutes.

Variation: With 4-6 thick pork chops.
Use 2 cups cranberry sauce,
cinnamon, nutmeg, salt and pepper.
Cover and bake at 350° for 1 hour.

The cranberry is one of the Heath
family (Ericaceae). The family includes
many plants, among them are the
blueberries, huckleberries and
bilberries.

Sailors from Canada and America ate cranberries, stored in fresh water in barrels, to protect themselves from scurvy, much as the British sailors ate limes. Now, if the Britons became known as limeys, how come Canadians and Americans were not called crannies?

View of the WHALE FISHERY, &c. in Greenland

[53] From an engraving made in 1781, in the Macpherson Collection.

CHAMPAGNE PUNCH

1 fifth champagne, chilled
2 28oz bottles ginger ale, chilled
4 cups orange juice, chilled
1 32oz bottle, (4 cups) cranberry
   juice cocktail, chilled

Combine in large punch bowl with ice.
Serve at once in punch cups.

[58] THE GREENLAND WHALE FISHERY.
From an aquatint by Dodd, published in 1789 by Boydell, London, in the Macpherson Collection.

SPICED PARTY PUNCH

9 cups UNSWEETENED PINEAPPLE JUICE
9 cups CRANBERRY JUICE COCKTAIL
1 cup brown sugar ~ 4½ t. whole cloves
4 cinnamon sticks, broken in pieces

Wash 30-cup percolator well. Mix juices,
4½ cups water, and brown sugar. Place
spices in basket. Plug in and perk for
5 minutes, as for coffee. Makes 23 cups.

GRANVILLE GRILL SAUCE

Combine one 10½oz can Tomato puree, one cup jellied cranberry sauce, two table-spoons vinegar, two tablespoons chopped onion and one tablespoon prepared horse-radish. Mix well.
Can be used for beef, shrimp or poultry. Makes about 2½ cups.

GRILLED CRANBERRY FRANKS

½ c. apricot preserves - ½ c. tomato sauce
½ c. jellied cranberry sauce - ¼ c. dry wh. wine
2 T. vinegar - 2 T. soy sauce - 2 T. honey
1 T. cooking oil — 1 t. salt - ¼ t. gr. ginger
2 pounds (20) frankfurters

Combine all except the franks. Score franks on the bias. Broil over hot coals, turning and basting with sauce.
Keep franks warm before serving by adding to heated sauce.

The word CRANBERRY is a contraction of two words, CRANE and BERRY. The pilgrims thought the blossom of the cranberry resembled the head of a crane. At least, that is how the folk-lore goes. Another version is that the fruit was a favorite food of the long-legged crane who liked swampy areas.

16

CORNELL CRANBERRY WASSAIL

1 c. sugar − ½ c. water − lemon slices
Cinnamon sticks − 4 cups red wine
2 cups cranberry cocktail
2 cups lemon juice, strained (10-12 lemons)

Combine sugar, water, 3 lemon slices
and 2 cinnamon sticks. Bring to boil
and boil gently 5 minutes. Strain.
Combine sugar, syrup, wine, cranberry
juice and lemon juice. Heat until
hot but do not boil.

When in serving bowl, garnish
with lemon slices.
Serve hot in mugs or punch cups.
Makes about 18 ½ cup servings.
Brandy can be added, to taste.

Note: This is an elegant Wassail and
it is said that it makes you feel
high above Cayuga's waters!

CRANBERRY RAISIN STUFFING

About 14 slices (14 cups) soft bread cubes
1 16 oz can whole cranberry sauce
4 T. butter − ½ c. raisins − ¼ c. sugar
1 t. salt − 1 t. lemon juice − ½ t. cinnamon
Toast cubes in 300° oven for 15 minutes. Toss
with melted butter. Add remaining items.
Toss till well mixed. Enough for 12 lb. bird.

17

CANADIAN BACON GOURMETS

1 can Cranberry Sauce - 2 T. light corn syrup
1 17oz can sweet potatoes - 1 T. butter (margarine)
1 T. brown sugar - ¼ t. gr. ginger
1 pound unsliced Canadian-style bacon

Combine cranberry and syrup and set aside.
Beat potatoes with butter, brown sugar and
ginger till fluffy - probably should use electric
mixer. Slice bacon into 12 pieces.

Spread half potato mixture on 6 of bacon
slices, in a 10x6x1½-inch baking dish. Cover
with remaining bacon and top with potatoes.
Drizzle cranberry mixture over each one.
Bake about 45 mins. at 350°, basting once
or twice with sauce in the dish.

SAUCY BERRY PUNCH

1½ c. sliced rhubarb — 1 c. chopped cranberries
1 c. sugar — ⅔ c. water — 1¼ c. pineapple juice
⅔ c. lemon juice — pink food coloring
cherries, plums or apricot halves in ice cubes
1 large bottle dry gingerale

Place fruit, water + sugar in pan and cook
until tender. Strain. Add pineapple and
lemon juice. (Tint if needed). Chill well.
Before serving pour over fruited ice
cubes. Add gingerale.
Variation: Omit fruited ice and use
Cranberry Rocks.

FERRY FIZZ

2 jiggers cranberry juice cocktail
1 jigger dry gin - 1 teaspoon lime juice
Combine, shake, and pour over ice.

YANKEE SQUARES

½ c. soft butter — 1 c. flour — 2 eggs
2 t. icing sugar — 1 c. white sugar
⅓ c. flour — ¼ t. salt — 1 t. baking powder
1 t. almond flavoring — ⅓ c. chopped raisins
½ c. coconut, shredded — ½ c. almonds
⅔ c. CRANBERRY SAUCE

Mix butter, 1 c. flour and icing sugar.
Spread in greased 8" square pan.
Beat eggs thoroughly and add sugar,
sifted dry ingredients and almond.
Stir in everything else and spread
mixture over bottom layer.
Bake at 350° for 40 mins. Cool and top
with your favorite icing.

CRANBERRY SPRING

2 cups Cranapple drink, chilled
1 pint lemon sherbet, softened
Mix well in blender, about 30 seconds.
Serve immediately in frosted glasses.
Garnish with lemon peel twists.

NORTH MOUNTAIN
COLDSLAW

Combine ¼ c. sliced cranberries, 1 T. honey
and 1 t. celery seed; let stand 15 minutes.
Add ¼ c. mayonnaise and 1 t. vinegar.
Pour over 3 cups shredded cabbage.
Season with salt.
Variation: Add juice from canned fruit

BAKED RUM CRANBANS

¼ c. butter   —   1 T. lemon juice
4 med. bananas, peeled, and
            halved crosswise
¼ c. packed brown sugar — light rum
½ c. heavy cream — 1 T. Confectioner's Sugar
1 c. finely chopped cranberries

Melt butter with lemon juice in baking
dish in 350° oven. Place bananas in
pan, turn to coat with butter + lemon.
Add cranberries. Sprinkle with br.
sugar and bake 20 mins.
Sprinkle with 2 T. rum and bake
1 min. longer. In small bowl beat
cream with Confectioners' sugar and
1 T. rum, until stiff peak stage.
Serve over warm cranberry-banana.

CRANBERRY- MAPLE GLAZE

2 c. fresh cranberries — 1/2 c. maple syrup
1 c. thick apple sauce — 1 t. grated lemon rind
Dash ground ginger.
Baste Pork roast twice with glaze.

CRANBERRY- HAM ROLLS

1/4 c. margarine   1/4 c. minced onion
1/4 c. chopped celery   2 c. cooked rice
8 slices boiled ham (1/8" thick)
1 can jellied cranberry sauce
1/2 c. packed brown sugar
salt and pepper to taste

Melt margarine in small saucepan.
Add onion and celery and saute
until soft. Remove from heat and
stir in rice and seasonings.
Divide rice mixture among ham
slices and roll up. Fasten each
with a toothpick and arrange in
greased shallow baking dish.
Crush cranberry sauce, add
brown sugar and mix. Spoon
over ham rolls and bake at
350° for 20 to 30 minutes.

CRANBERRY FOG

Combine 4 cups low-calorie chilled cranberry cocktail with ¼ c. lemon juice and 1 egg white. Shake well with crushed ice until foamy. Serve at once.

ORANGE-CRANBERRY BREAD

1 cup white sugar	chopped nuts
½ teaspoon salt	1 cup cranberries
½ " baking soda	2 " flour
1 egg - unbeaten	2 T. shortening
1½ teaspoon baking powder	Juice and grated rind of 1 orange

Mix dry ingredients together. Put juice, + orange rind in measuring cup. Add shortening, then fill cup to ¾ mark with boiling water. Add to dry mixture. Add unbeaten egg, cranberries and chopped nuts.
Bake in greased pan for 1 hour.
Stand 24 hours before slicing.

CRANBERRY GRILLED HAM

Beat together:
1 can jellied cranberry sauce, ⅓ c. steak sauce, 1 T. br. sugar, 1 T. cooking oil and 2 t. prepared mustard. Slash fat edge of 1 cooked ham slice about 1 inch thick. Broil over slow coals about 20 minutes. Brush with glaze last 15 minutes. (Broil each side about 20 minutes) Serves 4.

THREE-FRUIT SHERBET

Combine 1 chunked banana, 1 can jellied cranberry sauce, 1 can drained pineapple chunks, 1 cup whipping cream and 6 drops red food coloring. Switch blender on and off till well blended. Pile into 9x5x3-inch pan. Cover and freeze. Scoop into sherbet dishes.

CRANBERRY-ORANGE PETITS FOURS

Cut 1 12 oz loaf pound cake in 12 slices. Cut each slice in half vertically. Spread half the slices with about 1 Tablespoon CRANBERRY-ORANGE RELISH. Top with remaining slices. Brush sides and tops of petits fours with ¾ cup sweetened condensed milk. Sprinkle ¾ cup almonds, finely coated over surface.
Place on ungreased baking sheet. Bake 375° for 10-12 minutes. Remove from sheet and cool. Top with sweetened whipped cream.
Sometimes I cut the cake in 14 slices!

BOG BERRY SAUCE

— Place 2 c. cranberries in bowl, add 1 T. sugar and mash. Add grated rind of 1 orange. Refrigerate. Beat 1 T. butter. Add 1½ c. powdered sugar slowly, working in well. Now add 1 egg white, beaten stiff. Just before serving, combine with mashed berries.

SPICY CRANBERRY MUFFINS

Sift together 2 c. flour, ¾ c. sugar, 3 t. baking powder, 1 t. salt, ¾ t. gr. cinnamon and ¼ t. gr. nutmeg. Stir in ¼ c. chopped walnuts. Set aside. Combine 2 beaten eggs, ⅔ c. milk and ⅓ c. cooking oil. Add to dry mixture. Fold in 1½ c. cranberries, chopped, and 1 c. whole wheat flakes. Fill muffin pans ⅔ full. Sprinkle with 2 T. sugar and ¼ t. cinnamon mixture. Bake at 400° 20-25 minutes. (Makes 18)

COCONUT FRUIT BALLS

1   cup pitted prunes - ½ cup raisins
¾   cup dried apricots - ½ cup walnuts
1   8 oz pkg. pitted dates - ¼ cup sugar
1   cup cranberries
¼   cup orange juice concentrate, thawed
1   3½ oz can flaked coconut

Pour boiling water over prunes and apricots. Stand till cool, then drain. Coarsely chop fruits and nuts. Add sugar and orange juice. Form into balls, using about 2 teaspoons mixture for each one. Roll in coconut. (5 doz.)

GRANVILLE COMPOTE

1 pkg. dried apples (sliced)
2 cups cranberries
1 cup light brown sugar

Combine apple slices with 2½ cups water in a 2 qt. saucepan. Bring to boil. Reduce heat and simmer, covered 5-10 mins. Remove and spoon into medium bowl. In same saucepan, combine berries, sugar and 1¼ cups water. Bring to boil, stirring until sugar is dissolved. Cook till berries pop.
Stir apples into cranberry mixture. Bring to boil. Reduce heat and simmer, covered, stirring often. Continue about 10 minutes.
Pour into serving pan/bowl. Chill. Serve as a relish or compote.

HOT CRANBERRY WINE

1 32 oz bottle cranberry juice cocktail
2 cups water - 1 cup sugar - 12 whole cloves
4 inches cinnamon - Peel of ½ lemon, in strips
2 fifths dry red wine - ¼ c. lemon juice

Combine cranberry juice, water, sugar, spices and lemon peel. Simmer until sugar dissolved and bring to boil. Then simmer uncovered 15 minutes. Strain. Add wine and lemon juice. Heat but do not boil. Sprinkle nutmeg on top of each cup. Makes 14 cups.

CRANBERRY CREAM SANDWICH

½ cup cream cheese — 1 t. lemon juice
1 " chopped cranberries — 1 t. almond
Lettuce
Boston Brown Bread

Spread thinly on every slice and
put together with crisp lettuce between.

SVENGALI TOMATOES

Combine 1 16oz can tomatoes, cut up,
¼ cup C.-O. Relish, 2 Tablespoons light raisins,
1 Tablespoon sugar, ½ teaspoon ginger,
dash salt and ¼ teaspoon cayenne. Simmer
8-10 mins. Serve warm or chilled with
meat, poultry or game. (Makes about 2 cups.)

NOVA SCOTIA CIDER
(with CRANBERRY)

1 - 32-oz bottle (4 cups)
      CRANBERRY JUICE
4 cups apple cider
1 12-oz can apricot nectar
Several drops red food coloring
6 inches stick cinnamon
½ teaspoon nutmeg
1 cup rum
4 Tablespoons butter

Combine all except rum and butter.
Boil. Then simmer 10 mins. Remove from
heat. Add rum and butter, stirring until
butter melts. Serves 10.

GRANVILLE GROG

1 - 32 oz. bottle cranberry cocktail
3 cups grape juice
1 cup grapefruit juice
1 lemon - (cut in thin slices)

Combine and boil. Reduce heat.
Simmer 10 mins. Remove lemon
slices. Serve hot in mugs.

CRANBERRY CHILLER

1 jigger cranberry cocktail
1 oz. lemon juice — 1 jigger vodka
1 heaping teaspoon powdered sugar
Shake with ice. Pour unstrained into
glasses. Fill with sparkling water and
serve.

CRANBERRY CHEWS

2 eggs
3/4 cup sugar
1 T. lemon juice
1/4 t. nutmeg
Confectioners' Sugar
  (sifted)

1 1/2 cups biscuit mix
1 cup chopped pecans
1 can (8 oz) jellied
  CRANBERRY SAUCE
  (chilled and cubed)

Beat together first four ingredients
till light and fluffy. Stir in biscuit mix.
Gently fold CRANBERRY cubes into
batter along with nuts. Spread in
greased and floured 13x9x2-inch pan.
Bake 20-25 mins. (350°). Cool. Sprinkle
with sifted Confectioners' sugar.
Cut into bars.

CRANBERRY ORANGE SAUCE

2 cups sugar - ½ cup water
½ " orange juice- ½ " slivered almonds
1 lb. cranberries - 1 t. grated orange peel

Combine all except almonds. Cook, uncovered, 10 minutes, stirring once or twice. Cool. Cover and refrigerate. Serve with orange twist. MAKES 4 CUPS.

BAKED CRANAPPLE

6 medium firm red baking apples
2 cups cranberry sauce
1 cup water

Preheat oven to 350°. Wash and core apples. Starting at stem ends, pare apples one-third way down. Arrange in shallow casserole with pared sides up. Combine sauce with water and slowly pour over apples. Bake ½-1 hour basting frequently until apples are tender.

SPICY CRANPEACH SAUCE

1 16-oz can cling peach slices
1 cup sugar   - ¼ cup vinegar
1 t. whole cloves - 3 inches cinnamon
2 cups (½ lb.) cranberries

Drain peaches, keeping ⅔ c. syrup. Combine sugar, vinegar and spices with syrup. Bring to boil. Add cranberries. Boil without stirring until berries pop. Add peaches. Cool. Cover and refrigerate. MAKES 3 cups.

WHAT does the kitten say? "Mew, mew, mew!"
She shall have some nice milk, warm and new.

CRANBERRIE NUT TWIST

1 pkg. hot roll mix - 2 T. butter
½ cup chopped nuts - ¾ cup sugar
2 cups cranberries, coarsely chopped
1 teaspoon ground cinnamon
1 cup Confectioners' sugar
Cranberry juice cocktail

Prepare hot roll mix. Let dough rise in warm
spot till double, about 40 minutes. Punch
down. Roll out on lightly floured surface,
to 15 x 10 inch rectangle. Brush with butter.
Sprinkle with nuts, sugar, cinnamon and
cranberries. Roll up jelly-roll fashion.
Seal ends. Place seam side down on
greased baking sheet. Coil dough.

Let rise till almost double. Bake at 350°
for 35-40 minutes. Mix Confectioners'
sugar with cranberry juice to make
thin glaze. Brush over warm bread.
Makes a welcome holiday gift.

Green's Gourmet

Blend ¾ c. sugar, 1 T. unflavored gelatin and ½ t. salt in saucepan. Stir in 1 c. cranberry juice and 1 can whole cranberries. Cook slowly till boiling. Remove and chill a bit. Fold in ½ c. sour cream.
Turn into Graham cracker crust. Chill overnight. Stir 2 T. Confectioners' sugar into ½ c. sour cream and spoon atop.

BURGUNDY MARION - (PIE)

Boil together about 15 minutes:
1 ½ c. cranberries
1 ½ c. blueberries
1 ½ c. sugar ⌐ 1 c. water
Mix 2 T. corn starch in small amount of water. Pour into fruit to thicken and add dash of salt. Place in cooked shell. Chill.
Serve with whipped cream or ice cream.
A variation is to add some finely chopped berries to the whipped cream.

CRANBERRY DAIQUIRI - Cut 1 frozen block strawberries into 6-8 chunks. Combine in blender with 2 cups cranberry juice, and ¼ cup lemon juice. Add ¾ cup RUM. Serve over ice.

HAM and ASPARAGUS

1 slice ham per serving - ½"-1" thick
Top each slice with hot cooked frozen
asparagus. Spoon cranberry sauce
over top. Cover with sharp cheddar
cheese. Broil until cheese melts.
Serve with your favorite tossed salad
and muffins.

FUNDY FISH FILLETS

6 fresh fillets or 2 lbs. frozen fillets
    2 T. chopped onion
    ⅓ cup uncooked grain rice
    2 T. butter

Sprinkle fillets with salt and pepper. Cook
onion, rice and butter until browned, 5-8 mins.
Add:
    1 cup water
    1½ t. lemon juice
    1 chicken bouillon cube
    Pinch of salt
Boil and stir to blend. Cover. Cook over
low heat till liquid is absorbed and
rice is fluffy, 20-25 mins.
Stir in: 1-(3oz) can chopped mushrooms
      ½ cup jellied, mashed
         CRANBERRY SAUCE
Spread on fillets. Roll and place in greased
9x9x 2-inch dish. Brush with 2 T. melted
butter. Bake 25-30 mins. (350°).

Top with special Fundy Fillet Sauce (pg.53)

33

CRANBERRY APPLE SAUCE MOLD

Combine 1 16oz can dietetic-pack applesauce and 1 4-serving low-calorie
raspberry gelatin. Cook till dissolved.
Stir in 1 cup low-calorie cranberry
juice. Pour into 6 individual molds
or a 3-cup mold. Chill till firm.

MERINGUE SQUARES with CRANBERRY

1½ cups Vanilla wafer crumbs
4 T. butter — 4 T. sugar — 4 egg whites
½ c. sugar — 1 can cranberry sauce
1 2-2½oz pkg. dessert topping mix
Combine butter, crumbs and 2T. of sugar
Mix and spread firmly in 9x9x2-inch pan.
Beat egg whites until stiff and add sugar.
Swirl meringue over crumb mixture.
Bake at 325° for 12-15 minutes. Cool.
Spread cranberry sauce over meringue.
Prepare dessert topping and spread
over cranberries. Chill. Serves 9.

CRANBERRY-APPLE FLIP

2 c. cranapple drink — 1 egg white
¼ c. cherry brandy — 2 T. lime juice
2 t. sugar — 2 ice cubes

Combine all ingredients in
blender. Blend at high speed
for 30 seconds. Pour into glasses
and serve immediately.
Serves 2.

CRANBERRY GRAPE SALAD

2 cups cranberries   - ¾ cup sugar
1 " seeded halved grapes (red)
2 " miniature marshmallows
½ " whipped cream   - ¼ cup walnuts

Grind cranberries, coarse. Stir in sugar.
Cover, chill overnight. Drain, pressing
lightly. Add grapes, nuts, marshmallows
to well-drained cranberry mix. Before
serving, fold in whipped cream. Garnish
with lettuce and grape clusters.

GLAZED CRANBERRY LEMON BREAD

4 T. butter — ¾ c. sugar — 2 eggs
2 t. grated lemon peel — 2 c. sifted flour
2½ t. baking powder — 1 t. salt
¾ cup milk — 1 cup chopped cranberries
½ cup mixed candied fruits and peels
½ cup chopped walnuts
2 t. lemon juice   — 2 T. sugar

Cream butter and ¾ c. sugar till fluffy.
Add eggs and lemon peel, and beat well.
Sift together dry ingredients, except
sugar. Add this to creamed mixture
with milk, beating constantly till
smooth. Stir in berries, fruits and
peels, and nuts. Pour into greased pan
9 x 5 x 3-inch. Bake at 350° for 55-65
minutes. Let cool 10 minutes. Remove
from pan.
Combine lemon juice and 2 T. sugar.
Spoon over top. Wrap. Store overnight.

CRANBERRY-TOMATO SOUP

Combine 1 10¾oz can condensed tomato soup with ½ cup dairy sour cream. Stir in 2 cups cranberry juice cocktail and 2 Tablespoons lemon juice. Heat but do NOT boil. Pour into your favorite mugs and garnish with sour cream, if desired.

SKILLET CRANBERRY BARBECUE

½ c. chopped onion - 1 c. catsup
2 T. butter(margarine) - ¼ c. brown sugar
½ c. cranberry sauce - 3 T. vinegar
1 T. Worcestershire sauce - 1 T. mustard
1 12 oz can luncheon meat, in julienne strips
                Hot cooked rice

Cook onion in butter until tender but not brown. Stir in catsup, cranberry, sugar, vinegar, w. sauce, prepared mustard and meat. Simmer, uncovered, 15 minutes. Serve over hot cooked rice. Serves 6.

CRANBERRY STUFFED VEAL

About 1 pound veal, put through meat tenderizer, and cut into 8 very thin slices. On each slice place 1 very thin slice cooked ham. In centre of each put about 2T. cranberry sauce. Fold in half with ham inside and pat edges to seal.

Brown meat in butter on both sides. Add sprinkling of garlic salt. Place lemon slice atop. Combine 3 T. dry white wine and 2T. water; add to skillet. Simmer, covered, 5 minutes. Trim with perky parsley. Serves 4.

CRANBERRY-CHEESE FRUIT DESSERT

1 pkg. (10½oz) miniature marshmallows
1 can (20oz) crushed pineapple - drained
1 pkg. (3oz) cream cheese — 1 orange
1 cup heavy cream — 1 lb. cranberries
2 unpeeled apples, diced
2 cups halved grapes — 1 cup chopped nuts

Combine ½ pkg. marshmallows with
pineapple. Mix cheese with cream and
remaining marshmallows. Cover each
mixture and store in refrigerator over
night or until mallows are well softened.
Force berries through medium blade of
chopper. Wash orange, remove seeds
and white membrane and grind. (Do not
remove rind) Mix with remaining
ingredients. Beat cream mixture in
electric mixture till it resembles
whipped cream. Fold in pineapple and
cranberry mixtures. Chill. (Serves 10-12)

CRANBERRY TEA BISCUITS

2 c. sifted flour ⟶ 3 T. shortening
3 t. baking powder ⟶ ¼ t. baking soda
1 c. cranberries ⟶ Grated cheese
¼ c. sour cream ⟶ 1 egg

Sift together dry ingredients and cut in
shortening. Beat egg till creamy, add
cranberries, chopped, and sour cream and
add to first mixture. Roll out on floured
board and cut into biscuits. Place on
baking sheet and sprinkle with grated
cheese. Bake at 400° for 20 minutes.

Tea Time

CRANBERRY
Apple Ginger SQUARES

Combine 1 pkg. gingerbread mix and 1 can
applesauce. Stir in ½ c. chopped cranberries
and ¼ c. raisins. Spread in greased pan –
15½ x 10½ x 1-inch. Bake 15 mins. at 375°. Prepare
1 pkg. creamy white frosting mix, substituting
lemon juice (2 T.) for half the liquid.
Spread on cooled cake. Cut in squares.
(Makes 40)

CRANBERRY MINCEMEAT SPARERIBS

Add 1 c. water to 4 lbs. spareribs, cut up, in a shallow pan. Sprinkle with salt. Cover with foil, bake at 350° for 1½ hours. Drain. Dissolve 1 beef bouillon cube in ¼ cup boiling water. Combine with 1 cup prepared mincemeat and 1 can whole cranberry sauce. Pour over ribs. Bake, uncovered, 30-40 minutes more, basting occasionally. Makes 4-6 servings.

CRANBERRY BURGUNDY HAM

1 bone-in cooked ham
   (10-14 pounds)
1 can cranberry sauce
1 cup brown sugar
½ cup burgundy
2 t. prepared mustard
whole cloves

Place ham, fat side up, in shallow roasting pan. Score in diamond pattern. Stud with cloves. Bake at 325° about 3 hours. (130°)
In saucepan, combine remaining ingredients. Simmer, uncovered, 5 minutes. During last 30 minutes in oven, spoon half of cranberry glaze over ham. Pass remaining as a sauce. (About 2⅔ cups glaze.) Makes about 20-28 servings of ham.

CRANBERRIE COTTAGE COOLER

Combine equal parts white wine and
cranberry juice cocktail. Serve
over ice.

CRANBERRY-CHEESE PIE

1. In 9 x 3 inch springform pan mix
   3/4 cup graham cracker crumbs and
   3 Tablespoons melted butter.
   Press firmly in pan.
2. In small saucepan, sprinkle 2 envelopes
   unflavored gelatin over 2 cups cranberry-
   juice cocktail until dissolved. Set aside.
3. Whip 2 cups heavy cream in small bowl.
4. In large bowl, beat 4 8oz pkgs. cream
   cheese and 1 cup sugar until smooth.
   Gradually beat in gelatin mixture and 4t.
   lemon juice. Fold into whipped cream.
   Pour mixture into prepared pan and
   refrigerate about 4 hours.
5. Combine 2 cups cranberries and
   1 cup sugar and 3/4 cup cranberry
   juice and bring to a boil. Reduce
   heat and cook about 5 minutes.
   Meanwhile, in 1 cup measure sprinkle
   remaining 1 envelope gelatin over
   1/4 cup cranberry juice. Stir gelatin
   mixture into cranberry mixture.
   Chill till mixture mounds when dropped
   from spoon- 30 mins. Spoon over cream
   cheese mixture. Chill, about 45 mins.

CRANBERRY FRUIT TOPPING

½ each lemon and orange — 1 apple
¾ c. maple or maple-blended syrup
2 c. cranberries

Remove seed from lemon and orange.
Cut each half in 4 pieces. Core, peel
and quarter apple. Put syrup, apple,
cranberries and 2 pieces lemon and
orange in blender.
Add remaining citrus pieces. Cover
and blend about 30 seconds longer.
Serve as a topping for pancakes or
waffles. Makes about 2½ cups.

CRANBERRY-ORANGE SHERBET

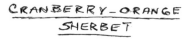

1 3 oz pkg. orange gelatin
1 cup boiling water
1 Tablespoon lemon juice
1 pint vanilla ice cream
1 orange, peeled and diced
1 can whole cranberry
   sauce (8 oz)

Dissolve gelatin in water. Stir in
lemon juice. Add icecream by spoonfuls, stirring till melted. Chill till
slightly thickened. Fold in orange
and cranberry sauce. Pour into pan
9x5x3-inch and freeze till firm. (1 quart)
Sometimes I substitute orange-
pineapple ice cream for a variation,
because it is my favorite.

CRANBERRY DROP COOKIES

2/3 c. shortening   1/2 c. cranberry juice
3/4 c. sugar   1/2 c. chopped cranberries
1 egg   2 t. grated orange rind
2 c. flour   1/2 t. baking powder
1/2 t. soda   1/2 t. salt

Glaze with Orange/Cranberry butter icing

Mix cookie ingredients. Drop on greased sheet. Bake at 350° until browned.

Icing: 2 1/2 T. soft butter
1 1/2 c. sifted Confectioners' sugar   } mix well
1 1/2 T. cranberry cocktail
2 tsp. grated orange rind

CRANBERRIE APPLE SAUCE

— Combine one 4-serving low-calorie raspberry gelatin with 1 lb oz can dietetic-pack applesauce. Cook and stir. Stir in 1 c. low calorie cranberry cocktail. Pour into 6 molds or one 3-cup mold. Chill till firm.

CRANBERRY-BANANA BREAD

Cream 4 T. butter and 1 c. sugar. Add 1 egg and beat well. Sift together 2 cups flour, 3 tablespoons baking powder, 1/2 teaspoon salt and 1/2 teaspoon cinnamon. Combine 1 cup mashed banana, 1/4 cup milk, and 1 teaspoon shredded orange peel. Add dry mixture and banana mixture alternately to creamed mixture. Stir in 1 1/2 cups cranberries and 1 cup chopped pecans. Bake 1 hour (350°). Remove. Cool.

BAKED CRANBERRY PEARS
(A weight-watcher delight)

4 fresh medium pears (pared, halved
                          and cored)
1 cup low-calorie cranberry juice
3 inches stick cinnamon
10 drops red food coloring

Use 1 quart casserole. Add all ingredients
and bring to boil. Bake, covered,
at 350° for 10 minutes. Turn pears,
bake, covered, another 10 minutes.
Turn pears, bake, uncovered, till
tender - about 5-10 mins. longer.
Remove cinnamon stick. Serve in
juice. Makes 8 servings.

CRANBERRIE SHERBET

In blender, combine 1 c. jellied cranberry sauce, 1 c. crushed ice, 2/3 c. evaporated milk, 1/2 c. sugar, 1 T. lemon juice, few drops red food coloring. Blend high till thick-about 2 mins. Freeze, covered, in 9 x 5 x 3 inch pan. Serves 3.

PEAR- CRANBERRY PIE

1 pkg. piecrust mix for 2-crust pie
1 cup cranberries — 5 large pears
1 cup sugar — 3 T. quick- tapioca
1/2 tsp. each gr. ginger and gr. cinnamon
2 T. butter, 1/2 c. water, milk, salt

Prepare pastry. Shape two-thirds of dough into a large ball and remaining into a small ball. Lightly flour board and rolling pin; roll out large ball into 11-inch circle. Line a 9-inch plate.

Crush berries with a potato masher in a large bowl. Peel, core and slice pears (thick) and add to berries. Stir in sugar, Tapioca, spices, salt and water. Spoon mixture into piecrust. Dot with butter.

Preheat oven to 425°. Roll small pastry ball into a rectangle, then cut for a lattice crust top. Brush top of strips with milk.

Bake about 1 hour. Serve warm or cold.

CRANBERRY SUMMER

Mix equal parts chilled cranberry cocktail and cold tea.
Serve in tall glasses with ice.
Add a crisp sprig of mint from the garden.

CRANBERRY ICE CREAM

¾ c. sugar — 2 T. all-purpose flour
1½ t. salt   — 2 c. milk

Combine sugar, flour and salt and gently stir in milk. Cook and stir over low heat till thickened.
Add small amount of cooked mixture to 2 beaten eggs. Mix well and add to hot mixture. Cook and stir 1 minute. Chill.
Stir in: — 2 cups whipping cream
          — 1 can cranberry sauce
          — 1 Tablespoon vanilla
Pour into freezer can of ice cream freezer. Pack crushed ice and rock salt around can using 6 ice to 1 salt. Turn dasher slowly till ice partially melts. Add more ice and salt. Turn till crank turns hard. Remove ice to below lid. Remove lid + dasher. Cover can with waxed paper. Replace lid. Fill freezer with more ice and salt. Cover freezer with heavy cloth or newspapers. Let ice cream ripen 4 hrs. before eating. Makes 1½ quarts.

ANNAPOLIS MIST

    1 jigger cherry brandy
        Cranberry juice cocktail
Pour brandy over crushed ice. Fill
with cranberry juice. Serve in old-
fashioned glasses.

FRUIT BOWL DENISE

2 bottles cranberry juice (8 cups)
6 envelopes unflavored gelatin — 1½ c. sugar
6 cups apple cider — 2 oranges, peeled, sliced
2 cans pear halves, drained (1 lb. size)
1 can sliced pineapple (1 lb. 4 oz.) - drained

1.- Make this a day ahead. Pour 4 cups
   cranberry juice into large bowl or
   5 qt. Dutch oven. Sprinkle gelatin and
   stand 5 minutes. Add sugar.
2.- Place mixture over low heat, stirring
   till both dissolve. Remove from heat.
3.- Add remaining cranberry juice and
   apple cider. Mix well.
4.- Pour 4 cups mixture into medium bowl and
   chill until slightly thickened — about 40 mins.
   Refrigerate remainder of gelatin mixture.
5.- Meanwhile, layer 5 orange slices in bottom
   of 4½ quart brandy snifter or glass bowl.
   Stand 7 orange slices against side of bowl.
6.- Pour thickened mixture over oranges and
   refrigerate till firm.
7.- Meanwhile, place 4 cups of remaining
   cranberry mixture in medium bowl. Set
   in a bowl of ice cubes until slightly
   thickened — about 40 minutes. (NEXT PAGE....)

48

FRUIT BOWL DENISE (CONTINUED)

8.- On the firm gelatin, stand pear
halves with cut sides against side
of bowl. Turn thickened gelatin
mixture into bowl and refrigerate
till firm- about 45 minutes.
9.- Cut 5 pineapple slices in half. Reserve
7 and cut rest into eighths.
10.- Chill remaining gelatin until slightly
thick.
11.- Arrange pineapple inside bowl on
Top of pears. (pineapple halves).
12.- Add cut up pineapple to remaining
gelatin and turn into bowl.
13.- Arrange orange slices on top.

Serve with whipped cream, topped
with CANDIED CRANBERRIES, or NUTS.

Although this festive fruit bowl can be
made ahead, it does take time. It
is worth the effort though - it looks
lovely - it tastes superb - it will be
the pièce de résistance of the occasion.

The Compleat Cook's Guide, published
in 1683, contained a recipe for
cranberry juice......

CRANBERRY CUSTARD PIE

1 can (15oz) sweetened condensed milk
2 cups fresh cranberries
¼ cup lemon juice   ½ cup water
2 egg yolks, beaten   1 cup whipping cream
1 cup sugar   1 T. sugar
½ t. vanilla   1 baked pastry shell

Combine milk, lemon juice, and egg yolks.
Spread evenly in shell. Chill 3-4 hrs.
Combine CRANBERRIES, the 1 cup sugar,
and water. Boil, then simmer 5 mins.
(uncovered). Drain. Put cranberries through
sieve or puree; cool.
Spread puree over custard layer. Whip
cream, the 1 T. sugar and vanilla. Spread.

Try the 1683
recipe for
cranberry juice:
"Put a teacupful
of cranberries
into a cup of
water, and mash them. In the
meantime, boil two quarts and
a pint of water with one large
spoonful of oatmeal and a very
large bit of lemon peel. Then
add the cranberries and as
much fine Lisbon sugar as shall
make a smart."

CRANBERRY LEMON FROSTING

1½ c. sugar — 1 t. corn syrup — 2 egg whites
6 T. cranberry juice — 2 T. lemon juice
¼ t. grated lemon rind
Combine in double boiler. Place over
boiling water. Beat until mixture peaks
and holds shape. Cool slightly and
spread.

Growth of Cranberry Production - Canada

1964 - 68	2,005,000	lbs
1969 - 73	7,773,000	"
- 74	9,414,000	"
- 75	12,485,000	"
- 76	14,400,000	"

BERRY NICE BAKED CRANBERRIES

This recipe should encourage more
frequent use of cranberries year round.
Simple to make - not too sweet - nice texture.

Measure any desired quantity cranberries.
Add sugar - ½ the quantity of cranberries.
Prepare oven - 350°.
A. - Spread berries in a single layer in baking
dish. Cover with the sugar. Cover dish
and bake in oven 15 minutes.
B. - Stir, recover, and return to oven for
another 15 minutes.
For extra elegant touch, add finely candied
ginger. Berries can be baked several
days ahead.

CRANBERRY COLLINS

    ½ cup CRANBERRY JUICE COCKTAIL
    1 jigger gin
    Tom Collins mix, chilled
Serve over ice or cranberry rocks

CRANBERRY SHORTCAKE

Sift together: 2 c. flour, 2 T. sugar,
3 t. baking powder and ½ t. salt.
Combine 1 beaten egg and ⅔ c. lt. cream.
Cut ½ c. butter into dry mixture and then
add egg and cream. Barely stir. Spread
in greased 8x11½inch pan, building up edges.
Bake in oven (450°) for 15-18 mins.

In saucepan, combine 2c. sugar and
1 c. orange juice. Boil 5 mins. Add
4 c. (1 lb.) fresh CRANBERRIES. Cook
5 mins. longer. Remove and cool. Then
remove shortcake from pan, cool on
rack for 5 mins. Split in 2 layers; lift
top off carefully. Butter bottom layer. Spoon
CRANBERRIES between layers and over
top. Garnish with whipped cream.

The Aylesford bog in Nova Scotia
now can harvest over 7000 lbs
daily. The old harvesting
methods caused at least a 25%
loss of crop.

For many years Massachusetts led the States in cranberry production.

HAM AND CHICKEN
FONDUE

½ cup orange juice
1 can cranberry sauce
Cooked ham or Chicken
    (cut in cubes)

1 T. cornstarch
1 T. br. sugar
¼ t. cinnamon

Blend juice and cornstarch. Add CRANBERRY sauce, br. sugar and cinnamon. Cook, stirring constantly, till thickens and bubbles. Keep sauce warm in fondue pot.

A Bronze age tomb in Denmark held a clay mug with a brownish sediment. Analysis proved it had been a drink using cranberries, bog myrtle and honey.

FUNDY FILLET
SAUCE

Melt 2 T. butter;
blend 2 T. flour.
Dissolve 1 chicken bouillon cube in ¾ c. boiling water. Add ½ c. milk and then add to flour mixture. Cook and stir till mixture thickens. Pour sauce over fish in serving dish. Top with ¼ cup slivered toasted almonds and Paprika.

CRANBERRY PECAN PIE

3 eggs   -   2/3 cup sugar
1 cup dark corn syrup - Pinch salt
6 T. butter, melted - 3/4 c. pecans
1 cup CRANBERRIES, chopped

Beat eggs to blend. Stir in corn syrup, sugar, butter, and salt. Sprinkle CRANBERRIES IN unbaked pastry shell. Pour syrup mixture over berries. Top with pecan halves. Bake 50-55 mins. (350°). Cool.

ALMOND CRANBERRY SAUCE

Mix 1 c. sugar and 1/2 c. water. Boil. Cook 5 mins. Add 2 cups cranberries. Cook 5 mins. Stir in 1/4 c. apricot preserves and 2 T. lemon juice. Cool. Add 1/4 c. toasted sliveved almonds. Serve over French toast or waffles topped with ice cream.

There are over 100 varieties of cranberries. Some have quaint names - Potter's Favorite, Budd's Blue, Centennial, Aviator.
Four varieties account for most cranberries in No. America.

It was nearly 100 years after the cranberry was cultivated, that the first can of cranberry sauce was packed. It was in the year 1912, in Hanson, Mass.

CRANBERRY GARNISH

Combine in large saucepan, 2 cups sugar, 4 cups cranberries, 1 cup water and 1/4 teaspoon each salt and baking soda. Bring to boil, cover, cook slowly 15 mins. Do not stir. Remove cover and cool. Refrigerate. Use as garnish for fruit cups and other desserts.

CRANBERRY-CHICKEN SPREAD

cranberry-orange relish
2 cans (4 3/4 oz) each chicken spread
2/3 cup dairy sour cream
1/4 " chopped golden raisins
1/4 "   "   toasted almonds
2 Tablespoons brandy (optional)
Chilled, sliced, nut bread
(Pinch of salt is optional)

Mix 1/3 cup relish and all ingredients except bread. Chill several hours. If longer chilling is desired, add nuts and brandy a couple hours before serving.
Garnish with relish and serve with nut bread. Makes 2 cups.

CRANHAM GLAZE

Dry mustard - 2 t.		Water _____ 2 T.	
Paprika _____ 1 t.		Lemon juice - 2 T.	
Ginger _____ 1 t.		Orange juice and	
Salt _____ 1/4 t.		rind — 2 oranges	
	CRANBERRY SAUCE — 1 cup		

Mix dry ingredients, juices and rind.
Stand about 1/2 hour to blend well.
Add cranberry sauce and heat slowly.
Cool and garnish with thin quartered
slices of half an orange.
Serve as sauce for cold sliced ham.

The traditional cranberry measure used
by pickers was a handled tin pail.
The pail was marked with 6 circular
grooves, each one marking off 1 quart.

SPICED CRANHAM GLAZE

1 c. cranberry sauce
2 T. cider vinegar
1/2 t. each dry mustard and gr. ginger
2 T. finely chopped pecans
1/4 t. Angostura bitters

Mix well and store covered in the
refrigerator. Makes about 1 1/4 cups.

Statistics Canada does not report
cranberry production from those
provinces with three or less
operators.

GRANVILLE SHORT RIBS

Beef short ribs   - 5½ to 6 pounds
Pineapple preserves - 12 oz jar (1 cup)
Cranberry sauce   - ½ cup
   ½ c. water - ½ c. chili sauce
   ⅓ c. vinegar - 2 t. salt - Dash pepper

Trim off excess fat; sprinkle meat with salt and pepper. Use Dutch oven. In about ½ c. water, simmer ribs till tender (2 hours) and cover, adding water if needed. Drain.
Coat ribs with mixture of remaining ingredients. Grill over slow coals about 20 mins. Turn and brush with sauce frequently. Serve remaining glaze hot, with ribs.

Both Canada and the United States had bumper crops in 1976 and the largest cranberry crop on record in 1977.

GRANVILLE PUDDING

Drain and cut up 1 16oz can peaches, reserving 2 Tablespoons syrup. Prepare 1 3¾ oz pkg. lemon whipped dessert mix. Add the reserved syrup to 1 3-oz pkg. softened cream cheese. Beat smooth. Gradually stir in whipped dessert. Chill till mixture mounds. Fold in peaches and 1 can jellied cranberry sauce, cubed. Chill in sherbet glasses. Makes 8 servings.

VALLEY VELVET

Mix and shake well, equal parts cranberry juice and rum. Serve on rocks or with soda. Garnish with thin wedge of lemon or lime.

Cranberries were described in 1614 by Captain John Smith. The earliest records of shipments to Europe were in 1550.

CRANBAN COFFEE CAKE

1½ cups sifted flour
½ cup sugar — 1 teaspoon salt
2 teaspoons baking powder
½ " baking soda
½ cup chopped walnuts
1 ripe banana (mashed)
½ cup milk — 1 beaten egg
¼ " melted shortening
1 can jellied cranberry sauce
16 pecan halves — ¼ cup sugar

Sift together first five ingredients. Stir in nuts. Combine banana, milk, egg and shortening. Add to dry mixture. Pour into greased 9x9x2-inch pan. Cut cranberry sauce into 4 slices; quarter each. Arrange atop batter. Top each quarter with pecan half. Sprinkle the ¼ cup sugar over all. Bake at 400° for 25-30 minutes.

The Algonquins of Wisconsin
and Canada, called the
cranberry, atoqua.

STUFFED BURGER BUNDLES

1 cup herb-seasoned stuffing mix
½ " cranberries, chopped
1 pound ground beef ← 1 T. catsup
⅓ cup evaporated milk
1 10½oz can condensed cream of
           mushroom soup
2 Teaspoons Worcestershire Sauce

Prepare stuffing, then add cranberries.
Combine meat and milk; divide in 5
portions. On waxed paper, pat each
portion to 6-inch circle.
Place about ¼ cup stuffing in centre
of each. Draw meat over stuffing to
make meat "balls", with stuffing inside.
Place in 1½ qt. casserole.
Combine remaining ingredients. Pour
over meat.
Bake, uncovered, at 350° for 45-50mins.

CRANBERRY SCOTIA

Mix well and serve over ice:
  cranberry cocktail — 3 ozs.
  Pineapple juice   — 1½ ozs
  Vodka   — 1½ ozs.

Garnish with orange peel twist.

CAPE COD CAKES (MUFFINS)

¼ c. shortening — ¼ c. sugar — 2 eggs
2 c. flour — 5 t. baking powder — 1 t. salt
⅔ c. milk — 1 cup CRANBERRY SAUCE

Cream shortening and sugar. Fold in
well-beaten eggs. Sift together flour,
baking powder and salt. Add to
creamed mixture alternately with milk.
Grease fluted muffin tins and fill
⅓ full, making dent in centre of batter.
Place 1 T. cranberry sauce in hole
and top with remaining batter till
⅔ full. Bake in hot oven (400°) about
30 minutes. Serve with cranberry
sauce. Makes about 12 medium muffins.

There are many legends about the
cranberry, and many of these come
from the Indian culture. One tale is
about a Medicine man who believed he was
more powerful than a local minister. So
he cast a spell and the Reverend was
stuck in quicksand. For two weeks the
clergyman was fed by a white dove
who brought red berries and dropped
them into his mouth. Some of the
berries fell to the ground and took
root and this was how the cranberry
bogs began.

The Cranberry is a native No. American fruit, of the genus Vaccinium L, from Latin vaccinus, meaning "of cows". One kind of Cranberry was the "cowberry"

CRANBERRY

BREAD PUDDING

1¾ c. scalded milk — ½ t. lemon extract
2 c. soft stale-bread cubes — ½ t. salt
¼ c. honey — 2 eggs, beaten — ½ t. vanilla
1 c. CRANBERRIES — Vanilla custard sauce
CREAM or Ice Cream

Mix all except cream and then pour into shallow 1½ qt. baking dish. Bake at 350° for 25 minutes, or until firm. Serve warm with cream. About 6 servings.

CRANBERRY CABBAGE MOLD

Soften 1 envelope gelatin in ½ c. cold water.
Add pinch of salt and stir over low
heat till gelatin is dissolved.
Beat 1 can jellied cranberry till smooth.
Stir in gelatin mixture, 1 c. shredded cabbage,
½ c. diced celery and 1 T. vinegar. Spoon
into 6 - ½ cup molds.   Chill.

The chemical composition of the
cranberry is:
   water (88 o/o) + 32 other ingredients.
   Energy value per 100 grams (3.5 ozs)
   is 26 calories.
Despite a popular notion, the ash of
the cranberry is slightly alkaline
and not acidic. There is a high
content of Vitamin C and this is
not diminished in storage.

CRANBERRY CRUNCH à la mode

1 c. uncooked rolled oats — ½ c. butter
½ c. sifted flour — 1 c. brown sugar
1½ c. cranberry sauce — Vanilla ice cream

Heat oven to 350°. Grease an 8 x 8 x 2-inch
pan. Mix oats, flour, sugar, and cut in butter
until crumbly. Place half of mixture in pan.
Cover with cranberry sauce, top with rest
of oat mixture. Bake 45 minutes. Serve
hot, cut in squares and top with ice
cream. Makes 6 - 8 servings.

62

"In the spring their glistening vines are like great carpets spread in the hollows." Jos.C. Lincoln, Cape Cod Yesterdays

CRANBERRY-ORANGE SQUARES - Dissolve 2 3oz raspberry gelatin in 2 c. boiling water. Stir in 2½ c. C.-O.Relish. Carefully stir in 1 cup lemon-lime carbonated drink. Pour into 8x8x2 inch pan. Chill till firm. Cut in squares.

Nova Scotia was the first province to cultivate the cranberry but with high tariff laws and changing economic conditions, the cranberry industry declined in the late 1800's.

CRANBERRY MINCE
COFFEE CIRCLE

2 cups flour	½ cup milk
¾ " sugar	½ " mincemeat
2½ t. baking powder	½ " ground cranberries
½ t. salt	1 egg, slightly beaten
⅓ c. shortening	Confectioners' Icing

Sift together dry ingredients. Cut in shortening - coarse crumbs. Combine egg, milk, mincemeat, and CRANBERRIES. Add to dry ingredients, mixing till flour is moistened. Spoon into well-greased 8-inch ring mold. Bake 30-35 mins. (375°). While still warm, drizzle with Confectioners' Icing.

CRANBERRY MARSHMALLOW FREEZE

Beat 1 can cranberry sauce into 1 7oz jar marshmallow creme. Turn into 9x5x3-inch pan and freeze. Whip ½ cup cream. Remove frozen mixture, break into chunks and add 1 T. lemon juice. Beat till fluffy. Fold in whipped cream. Freeze. Makes 1 quart.

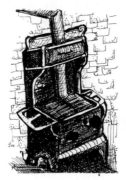

Cranberry Production
- Canada - 1975 -

Newfoundland	140,000 lbs
Prince Edw. Island	10,000 lbs
Nova Scotia	110,000 lbs
Br. Columbia	12,225,000 lbs
	12,485,000 lbs

CRANBERRY JUBILEE

1 cup sugar	2 cups cranberries
1½ " water	¼ " brandy
Vanilla ice cream	

Combine sugar and water in saucepan. Stir to dissolve sugar. Boil 5 mins. Add CRANBERRIES and bring to boil again. Cook 5 mins.
Turn into heat-proof bowl or blazer pan of chafing dish. Heat brandy. Ignite brandy and pour over CRANBERRY mixture. Blend into sauce. Serve immediately over ice cream. Makes 2½ cups.

BOG BERRY PUNCH

In punch bowl, combine two 32-oz bottles cranberry juice cocktail, chilled, and ½ cup grenadine syrup.
Just before serving, add two 12oz bottles cherry carbonated beverage, chilled, and two 12oz. bottles lemon carbonated beverage. Stir gently. Serve over cranberry rocks. Garnish with fresh mint sprigs. (14 cups)

ETTINGER SPECIAL

½ c. flour	1 c. dark brown sugar
½ t. salt	2 t. baking powder
3 eggs	1 c. chopped cranberries
2 t. vanilla	½ c. chopped walnuts
1 c. chopped, peeled apple	

Beat eggs and sugar together until creamy. Stir in sifted dry ingredients. Add vanilla, nuts, apple and berries. Mix well. Pour into large greased pie pan and bake 35 mins. at 350°. Cut into wedges and serve warm with ice cream.

PINK PINEAPPLE PUNCH

3 cups cranberry juice cocktail, chilled
1 cup pineapple juice, chilled
2 Tablespoons lemon juice
1 Tablespoon instant tea powder
2 7-oz bottles gingerale, chilled

Combine juices, and tea. Carefully stir in gingerale. Pour over ice. (Makes 6 cups)

HOT CRANBERRY SWIZZLE

3/4 c. brown sugar — 1 cup water
1/2 t. each cinnamon, allspice, cloves
1/4 t. salt — 1/4 t. nutmeg — 3 c. water
2 cans jellied cranberry sauce
4 cups unsweetened pineapple j.
Butter or margarine

Combine brown sugar, the 1 cup water, cinnamon
allspice, cloves, salt and nutmeg. Bring to boil.
Add cranberry sauce, beat till smooth.
Stir in the 3 cups water. Add pineapple juice.
Simmer, uncovered, about 5 minutes. Serve
in mugs and dot with butter. Makes 10 cups.

It's the berries! Cook with
CRANBERRY year round.

DECEMBER SHORTCAKE

2 c. biscuit mix — 2 Tablespoons sugar
1 beaten egg — 4 " butter, melted
2/3 c. light cream — 1 apple, cored, pared
1 8 oz crushed pineapple, drained
1 can whole cranberry sauce
1 cup whipping cream, whipped
Combine 1st 5 items and beat well. Spread in
greased pan. Bake at 450° for 15-18 minutes.
Remove and cool on rack for 5 minutes.
Combine fruit. Split cake in 2 layers.
Spoon fruit mixture between after
buttering bottom layer. Garnish with
whipped cream. Serve warm.
Note: chop apple before mixing. Variation is
to drop batter on baking sheet by spoonful.

CRANBERRY-PINEAPPLE JELLY

Combine 3 cups cranberry J. cocktail,
I cup unsweetened pineapple juice,
1/3 cup lemon juice and 1 3/4 oz. pkg. powdered
fruit pectin. Bring to boil. Then stir in 5 cups
sugar. Bring to rolling boil - hard for I min.
Stir constantly. Skim off foam. Pour
into 6 hot sterilized glasses. Seal.

BELLE ISLE COOLER

In large pitcher, combine ice cubes, halved
fresh strawberries, 4 cups low-calorie
cranberry cocktail (chilled) and 2 cups
low-calorie lemon-lime drink. Chill. (6 1/2 cups)

CRANBERRY-PRUNE RELISH

2 cups cranberry-orange relish
1 cup pitted prunes, chopped
1/2 lemon skin and all, chopped
1/3 cup Cointreau - or any orange-
        flavored liqueur
1/2 cup sugar
1 cup blanched almonds

Combine all ingredients except almonds
with I cup water in a saucepan.
Bring to boil and simmer -15-20 mins.-
or till thickened. Stir in almonds.
Cool and refrigerate - or pour into
sterilized jars and seal. Chill before
serving. Makes about 3 1/2 cups.

CRANBERRY CONFETTI PIE

1 envelope unflavored gelatin
1 Tablespoon sugar
1½ cups cranberry cocktail
1 3-oz pkg. lime gelatin
1½ cups boiling water
2 envelopes unflavored gelatin
2½ cups cranberry cocktail
1 9-oz carton frozen whipped
    topping, thawed
16 ladyfingers, split

Soften 1 envelope gelatin and sugar in the 1½ c. cranberry juice. Stir over low heat. Pour into 8x8x2-inch pan. Chill till firm. Dissolve lime gelatin in boiling water. Pour into 8x8x2-inch pan. Chill till firm. Soften 2 envelopes gelatin in the 2½ c. cranberry juice. Stir over low heat. Chill until slightly thickened. Fold in whipped topping.
Cut red and green gelatin into ½ inch cubes. Fold half the cubes into topping mixture. Line 10-inch pie plate with ladyfingers. Sprinkle with remaining gelatin cubes. Chill firm.

ZESTO DRESSING - (for weight watchers)
In blender, combine 1 c. dry-curd cottage cheese (or 1 c. drained cream-style), 3 T. skim milk, 1 T. lemon juice, 2 t. prepared horseradish, dash salt and sprigs parsley. Blend at high speed about 1 minute. Chill.

GRANVILLE CONSERVE

Mix following ingredients. Stand 10 mins.

4 c. cranberries   2 c. raisins
4 T. orange rind   1 T. lemon rind
2 T. lemon juice   ½ c. orange juice
6 c. sugar

Boil 10 minutes. Reduce heat. Simmer until thickened. Pour into sterilized jars and seal. (Makes 6 jars)

ANNAPOLIS SALAD
(fruit and cheese)

12 cups torn lettuce
8 oz sharp cheddar cheese
    (cut in thin strips)
½ cup sliced celery

Combine in large salad bowl.

Dressing:
⅔ cup salad oil
⅓ cup wine vinegar
½ cup sugar
2 teaspoons grated onion
1 teaspoon dry mustard
½ teaspoon salt

Coat lettuce, mix lightly with dressing. Toss. Top with:

2 oranges, peeled, cut in bite-size pieces
1 can jellied cranberry sauce, chilled and cubed
1 medium avocado, peeled and sliced

Toss gently. Pass remaining dressing.

DOUBLE BERRY SODA
3 cups cranberry juice cocktail
1 pint raspberry sherbet
1 12 oz bottle raspberry carb. drink
1 10 oz pkg. frozen raspberries,
   thawed. (optional)

Make soda as for Cranberry Soda.
Garnish with a spoonful of
raspberries.

FRUIT SALAD with sour cream
Drain 1 can mandarin oranges and 1 13½ oz
can pineapple tidbits. Combine with
1 c. coconut, 1 cup tiny marshmallows and
1 can jellied cranberry sauce, chilled and
cubed.
Fold in 1 cup dairy sour cream.
Chill overnight.   Makes 8 servings.

CRANBERRY SODA
4 cups cranberry-apple drink
1 pint vanilla ice cream
2 7oz bottles lemon-lime beverage

In each of 4 tall soda glasses, combine
a little of the cran-apple drink and
a spoonful of ice cream. Stir to
muddle. Fill glasses with several
small scoops ice cream. Slowly
pour in cran-apple drink till glasses
are ⅔ full. Resting bottle on rim
of glass, slowly pour carbonated
beverage to fill glasses. Stir gently.

MERRIE MELISSA (Pudding)

1½ c. flour — 2 t. baking powder
⅓ t. salt — ⅓ c. sugar — ½ c. milk
2 eggs, beaten — 1 T. butter, melted
1 cup fresh (or frozen) cranberries

Sift dry ingredients together. Combine milk, eggs and butter and add, stirring gently to make batter smooth. Fold cranberries in carefully, pour into well-greased molds (line bottoms with waxed paper). Cover and steam for 45 minutes. Serve warm with HARD SAUCE or BERRY SAUCE.

CRANBERRY FRITTERS

WASH desired amount of fresh, firm cranberries. Toss them in a bag with enough sugar to cover. Dip them in "fritter batter" and fry in deep fat (365°) for about 2 minutes. Serve with Confectioners' sugar and use as garnish, with hot or cold meats or with salads.

Fritter
Batter :

Sift together 1⅓ c. sifted flour, dash of salt, 2 t. baking powder, and 2 T. sugar. Add 1 well-beaten egg and ⅔ c. milk. Batter should be just thick enough to coat the berries.

CRANBERRY-RASPBERRY RING

Dissolve 1 pkg each (3 oz) raspberry and lemon gelatin, in 1½ c. boiling water. Stir in 1 10oz pkg frozen raspberries. Add 1 c. cranberry-Orange Relish. Chill till cold but not set. Carefully add 1 bottle (1 cup) lemon-lime carbonated drink. Stir gently. Chill. Then turn into 5-cup mold. Chill till firm.

Ground Ivy

CRANBERRY OPERA FUDGE

2 cups sugar ⌐ ½ cup milk
½ cup light cream ⌐ 1 t. vanilla
1 T. light corn syrup ⌐ ½ t. salt
1 T. butter ⌐ ½ c. chopped cranberries

Butter sides of heavy 2-qt. saucepan. Combine sugar, milk, cream, syrup and salt. Cook and stir over medium **heat** until mixture boils. Cook to soft-ball stage (238°). Quickly remove from heat and cool to 110° without stirring.
Add butter and vanilla. Beat till thick and loses gloss. Stir in berries quickly and spread in buttered pan 9x5x3-inch. Score in squares while warm. Cut when cool and firm. (Makes 2½ dozen pieces)

CRANBERRY - APPLE
ROLLS

1 pkg. hot roll mix
¾ c. warm water
¼ c. sugar
½ t. nutmeg
1 egg - ½ c. sugar
½ c. cranberries
1 apple - pared, chopped
¼ c. chopped walnuts
1 T. butter
Confectioner's Icing

Dissolve yeast in mix in the ¾ c. warm
water. Stir in the ¼ c. sugar, nutmeg, egg
and mix. Cover and chill thoroughly.
Roll out to 18"x10" rectangle. Cut in
eighteen 10" strips. Roll each into a "rope".
Coil loosely to form round balls.
On greased baking sheet, gently press each
centre and fill with 1 T. of CRANBERRY-
APPLE FILLING. Let rise in warm spot
30-45 mins. or until double. Bake 15 mins.
(375°). Drizzle with. C. Icing while
warm. Makes 18 rolls.

CRANBERRY-APPLE FILLING
In small saucepan, combine apple,
cranberries and the ½ cup sugar.
Cook and stir until apple is tender.
6 to 8 minutes. Remove from heat
and stir in nuts and butter. Cool
(See Cranberry-Apple Rolls for details)

CRANBERRY - COTTAGE CHEESE SALAD

Sprinkle 1 envelope gelatin over ¼c. water.
Cook and stir until dissolved. Cool slightly.
Stir in: 1 can cranberry sauce
     1 pkg (16oz) creamed cottage cheese
     Dash of salt
Chill about 10 minutes.
ARRANGE canned pineapple slices, one to a
dish, on lettuce (or on a platter). With ice-
cream dipper, scoop out jellied mixture and
place on each pineapple slice.
Top with whole plain or candied berries.

CRANBERRY RASPBERRY PIE

1 - 10oz. pkg. frozen raspberries
5 cups fresh cranberries
1½ cups sugar
3 tablespoons cornstarch
¼ teaspoon salt
(Pastry - 2-crust 9" pie.)

Drain raspberries and keep syrup. Add
enough water to syrup to make 1 cup.
Combine CRANBERRIES and syrup mixture in a large saucepan. Bring to
boil. Simmer 5 mins.
Combine sugar, cornstarch and salt.
Add to hot CRANBERRY mixture. Cook
quickly. Stir constantly until thickened.
Remove from heat. Stir in raspberries.

Fill pastry-lined 9" plate. Adjust top
crust. Seal and cut slits for steam.
Bake 35-40 mins. in 400° oven.

CRANBERRY-APPLE PUDDING
1 pkg. Zwieback — 8 large apples
1 heaping T. butter — 1 jar heavy cream
½ c. sugar   —   1 c. chopped cranberries
Roll out 1 pkg. Zwieback. Mix butter and
sugar with Zwieback and warm.
Alternate layer of crumb mixture in a
buttered loaf pan, with sliced pared
apples and cranberries (mixed). Continue
layers until none is left, ending with
top layer of crumbs.
(Dot with butter and pour batter over
fruit mixture for a variation).
Bake in a moderate oven (350°) 1 hour.
Serve with whipped cream.

CRANBERRY ROLY POLY
2 c. chopped cranberries* — ¾ c. sugar*
½ t. cinnamon* — 2 t. grated lemon rind* — 2 T. butter
1 recipe Baking Powder biscuit.
Combine.* Roll out dough - ¼" thick rectangle.
Spread with butter and mixture. Roll up as
for jelly roll. Wet edges and press. Place
in a cloth and tie loosely. Steam 1½ hrs.
Remove from cloth, slice and serve
with pudding sauce.

CRANBERRY FLAMBÉ - Combine 2 c. sugar, ½ c. water, ½ t. orange peel, ½ c. orange juice. Boil 5 mins. Stir in 2 c. cranberries. Boil. Simmer 5 mins. Blend 2 t. cornstarch with 2 T. cold water. Stir into hot mixture. Cook till thick. Pour into chafing dish. Heat ¼ c. brandy - pour over mixture - ignite. Spoon over vanilla ice cream.

CRANBERRY EATON (BREAD)

2 c. flour — 1 c. sugar — ½ t. soda
1 t. salt — 1 orange (juice and grated rind)
orange juice or water — 1 egg, beaten
½ c. dates, cut fine — 3 T. shortening
½ c. chopped nuts — ½ c. chopped citron peel
2 c. halved cranberries

Heat oven at 350°. Grease loaf pan - 9x5x3-inch. Halve berries and add ¼ cup sugar. Stand aside while sifting dry ingredients in a bowl, using ¾ c. sugar. Combine squeezed orange juice plus enough juice, (cranberry or orange) or water, to measure ¾ cup liquid. Add grated rind, melted shortening and beaten egg. Pour all at once into dry ingredients mixing just enough to dampen. Carefully fold in chopped nuts and cranberries and citron peel. Spread evenly in prepared loaf pan. Bake for 1 hour. Cool. This bread slices best if stored overnight. Can be wrapped in foil to freeze.

CRANBERRY SAUCE

Cook 2 cups cranberries with 2 cups water. In 5 minutes add 2 cups more of cranberries. When skins pop, strain and add sugar (2 cups). Boil 10-15 mins. Pour into dish and chill. Can be frozen.

CRANBERRY QUICHE
- 1 8" quiche -

½ c. cranberry sauce — 2 t. flour
½ c. COOKED meat (turkey, chicken or ham)
¾ c. grated Swiss cheese — 2 eggs
1 c. heavy cream — salt + pepper
Pastry for 1 8" pie shell
Finely chopped, toasted almonds

Line pie plate with pastry. Spoon cranberry sauce into bottom and sprinkle cooked meat on top. Mix cheese and flour and sprinkle over cranberry and meat.
In a bowl, mix eggs, heavy cream, salt and pepper and beat until smooth. Pour mixture into pie shell. Place on cookie sheet and bake in a moderate oven (350°) about 40 minutes.
Serve hot sprinkled with toasted almonds.

AUNT ANNA'S COFFEE CAKE

Cream 2/3 c. butter with 1 c. sugar. Add 2 eggs, one at a time, beating well. Mix 2 2/3 c. flour, 3 t. baking powder and 1 t. salt and add alternately with 1 c. milk. Beat until smooth. Add 2 t. cranberry syrup (or vanilla extract) and spread in greased 13 x 9 x 2 pan. Spread with CRANBERRY Topping then sprinkle with CRUMB Topping. Bake at 350° about 35 mins. Serve warm or cool.

CRANBERRY - CREAM CHEESE FROSTING

Soften 1 pkg. (3ozs) cream cheese in small bowl of electric mixer. Beat in 1/4 cup cranberry sauce. Add about 2 cups confectioners' sugar, beating until smooth and of spreading consistency.

TWANGY TARTS

4 c. sugar — 1/4 c. boiling water — salt
2 1/2 c. cranberries — 3 1/2 T. cornstarch
2 T. sugar — 1 t. lemon rind — 1 t. lemon juice

Make syrup and add berries. Cook until they burst. Mix cornstarch, sugar, salt, lemon juice and rind. Add to berries. Divide mixture among 12 pastry-lined tart shells. Make lattice tops or make plain fluted edges.

Bake in hot oven (400°) for 25-30 mins. Serve warm.

Booth Bay Pork Chops (Aunt Lill)

Simmer in a delicate wine sauce for an elegant skillet supper. Garnish with lemon slices and sprigs of parsley.

4 pork chops (1 inch) — 2 T. cooking oil
½ cup dry red wine — ½ c. honey
1 cup CRANBERRIES — 1 teaspoon salt

Brown chops in hot oil, and season with salt and pepper. Drain. Combine wine and honey; pour over chops. Cover and simmer 1 hour, adding cranberries about 10 minutes before end of cooking time. Makes 4 servings.

Ruby Red Salad

Bring 2 cups cranberry juice to a boil. Add 2 3oz pkgs raspberry gelatin and stir until dissolved.
Add to above: 1 can pineapple tidbits
½ cup port
½ cup water
On bottom of a 5-cup mold, arrange avocado slices (1 avocado, peeled). Cover with gelatin mixture and chill. Then chill remaining gelatin mixture and when partially set, fold in 1 cup diced pared apple and ½ cup finely chopped celery. Pour over avocado layer that is partially firm. Chill well. Unmold. Garnish with grapefruit sections and bibb lettuce.

CRANBERRY ROCKS

Fill ice cube tray with cranberry
juice cocktail.
Freeze and presto-cranberry rocks!
Add rocks to your favorite fruit
juice or iced tea — they sparkle.
Great in soft drinks or with rum,
gin or vodka.
Kids love them too - frozen on sticks.

CONNOR'S
SWEET and SOUR BEEF STEW

mix well and coat 2 lbs. stewing beef
with following:
3 T. flour — dash salt — ½ tsp. each
   celery salt, garlic salt, ginger
Brown in Dutch oven, using 3 T. oil.

Stir in   1 can Tomatoes (28 oz)
          ½ cup Molasses
          ⅓ cup red wine vinegar
          2 medium sliced onions
Cover and simmer 2 hours

Add   6 carrots
          1 cup cranberries
          ½ cup raisins
Cook until tender (15 minutes)
Serve immediately or freeze

   An elegant/simple dinner served
   with thick slices country bread
   and red wine and candlelight.

THE BIVOUAC.

London: Hurst & Blackett 1855

Rice Stuffing with Cranberries and Mushrooms

Cook 1 16oz pkg. long-grain rice as directed.

Over low heat, in ¾ c. hot butter (or margarine) cook 1½ lb. mushrooms, sliced, 4 cups fresh chopped onion, 2 cups uncooked cranberries, 2 cups diced celery and ¾ cup chopped celery leaves, until celery is tender. (About 15 minutes). Stir in rice. Add 2 tsp. salt and 1½ tsp. poultry seasoning plus 1 tsp. summer savory.

CRANBERRY-SHRIMP DIP

Force 2 cups cranberries and 1 medium onion through food chopper. Add 1 tsp. salt, 1/4 tsp. cider vinegar, 1 cup each sugar and chili sauce. Heat to boil. Reduce heat. Simmer about 10 minutes. Stir constantly. Add 1 tsp. Worcestershire sauce and 1/4 tsp. hot pepper sauce.

CRANBERRY DIP

2 c. cranberry j. cocktail
3 T. cornstarch — 1/4 c. cider vinegar
1/4 c. sugar — 1/2 t. salt
2 chicken bouillon cubes

Blend some cranberry juice with cornstarch. Put remaining juice with remaining ingredients in pan. Stir in cornstarch and cook, stirring, until smooth and thickened.

MEATBALLS with CRANBERRY DIP

1 1/2 lbs. meat-loaf mixture — 2 eggs
1/2 c. cranberries — 1 T. soy sauce
1 can water chestnuts, drained and chopped
1/2 t. salt — 1/4 t. pepper
1/2 c. minced onion — 1/4 c. margarine

Combine all except margarine. Mix well and shape into tiny balls. Brown in hot margarine in skillet. Spear meatballs with toothpicks and serve with Cranberry Dip. About 100 meatballs.

RICE PUDDING MOLD

A glamorous version of an old
  Nova Scotian favorite.

In saucepan, combine 1½ cups water with
½ c. uncooked long-grain rice and ½ t. salt.
Bring to boil and then simmer 15 minutes.
In small saucepan, combine:
    1 envelope unflavored gelatin
    1 can cranberry sauce - ½ cup Kirsch
Stir over low heat until dissolved.
Stir into rice mixture.
Beat 2 egg yolks with ¼ cup sugar
Stir small amount rice mixture into yolks.
Then mix all with rice mixture.
Cook and stir over low heat 2-3 minutes.
Fold in ¼ cup chopped candied fruits + peels.
Chill till mixture mounds.
Beat egg whites till frothy. Gradually add
¼ cup sugar until stiff peak stage. Fold
1 cup whipped cream and egg whites
into rice mixture. Turn into tall
6-cup mold. Chill overnight.
Unmold and serve with Cranberry Rum
Sauce.

Do not top the mold with the sauce.
Put sauce in small dish nearby and
serve molded pudding on cake stand
or compote for effect.

CANDIED CRANBERRIES

½ c. firm cranberries
½ c. sugar — ½ c. water

Wash and dry berries and prick each one with a needle. Boil sugar and water till syrup spins a thread (234°). Add berries and cook syrup until it forms a hard ball in cold water.

Lift berries from syrup, remove to wax paper and let stand until well dried. Roll in granulated sugar. Use like candied cherries.

CRANBERRY CHOCOLATE TORTE

1 quart vanilla ice cream
1 can whole cranberry sauce
1 pkg. 2-layer-size devil's food cake mix
1 2 or 2⅛ oz pkg. dessert topping mix

In chilled bowl, stir ice cream to soften. Quickly stir in half of cranberry sauce. Spread evenly in foil-lined 9 x 1½-inch round pan. Cover and freeze 2-3 hrs. Prepare cake. Bake in 2 9 x 1½-inch round pans. Cool.

Just before serving,* place one cake layer on serving plate. Place ice cream atop cake; top with second layer. Prepare topping. Fold in remaining cranberries. Frost cake. Serve.

* You can fill, frost and freeze cake ahead of time. After cake is frozen, wrap and return to freezer till serving time.

Cranberry sauce is also used
in sandwiches. This is said
to be a popular snack or
noonday lunch among the
people living in the Pine Barons
region of New Jersey. (National
Geographic magazine)

CHURCH POINT CRÊPES

1 c. sifted flour — 1 T. sugar — 2 eggs
1½ c. milk — 2 t. each grated orange peel
½ t. vanilla   and orange juice
¼ t. salt — 2 4oz whipped cream cheese
⅔ c. chopped pecans — 2 T. cornstarch
2½ c. cranberry cocktail — ½ c. sugar
½ c. orange-flavoured liqueur

Combine flour, sugar, milk, eggs, ½ t. orange peel,
juice, vanilla and salt. Beat till smooth.
Lightly grease 6-inch skillet. Heat and remove.
Spoon in about 2 spoonfuls batter. Rotate pan
to spread evenly. Brown one side only.
Invert pan over paper towel to remove.
Repeat with occasional regreasing.
Spread unbrowned side with cream cheese
and sprinkle with nuts. Roll up. Place corn-
starch in blazer pan and stir in cranberry
juice. Cook quickly, stirring constantly.
Stir in ½ c. sugar, peel and liqueur.
Add filled crêpes. Heat through.
If desired, cover and refrigerate crêpes
with filling. At serving time, heat in
sauce as in recipe. Makes 9 servings.

FRUIT BLENDER SHAKE

1 c. cranberry cocktail — 6-8 drops red
1 c. vanilla ice cream — food coloring
1 orange, peeled and sliced or 2 halved peaches

Combine all but ice cream. Blend at high speed until smooth. Add ice cream. Blend slightly. Serve immediately. (Makes 2 cups)

CRANBERRIE RICE

1 cup cooked rice — 2 Tablespoons sugar
1 can cranberry sauce, drained
1 can crushed pineapple, drained (8½oz)
1 cup miniature marshmallows
1 cup whipping cream, whipped

Combine all except whipped cream. Then fold in whipped cream. Chill. (8 servings)

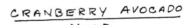

CRANBERRY AVOCADO
MOLD

2 3oz pkgs. raspberry gelatin
2 cups boiling water
1½ " cold water
1 " ground cranberries
½ " sugar - Dash salt
1 avocado, peeled & cubed
¼ cup chopped walnuts

Dissolve gelatin in boiling water, then add cold water. Chill until partially set. Combine ingredients. Fold into gelatin. Pour into 6½-cup mold. Chill till firm. Unmold on lettuce leaves.

CRANBERRY COTTAGE CAKE

1 cup CRANBERRIES (chopped)
¼ " sugar
2 " biscuit mix
2 Tablespoons flour

½ cup sugar
3 tablespoons shortening
½ cup milk
1 egg
1 teaspoon vanilla

CRANBERRY cake sauce

Sprinkle CRANBERRIES with ¼ cup sugar. Combine biscuit mix, flour, and the ½ cup sugar; stir in shortening, milk, egg and vanilla till smooth. Stir in CRANBERRIES. Pour into greased pan - 9 x 9 x 2 - inch. Bake 30 - 35 mins. - 350°.

Serve with Cranberry Cake Sauce
Combine ½ c. sugar, 2 T. cornstarch, and 1½ c. cranberry juice cocktail. Cook. stir until thickened. Cook 2 mins. more. Stir in ¼ c. butter till melted. 9 servings.

LUNENBURG SAUERBRATEN

In Dutch oven, brown 3½-4 lb. beef
rump roast, on all sides. Season
with salt and pepper.
Add: 2 cups CRANBERRIES
    1   "   chopped onion
    ½   "   chopped celery
    ½   "   water
Cover tightly - cook slowly 2 - 2½ hours.
Add water to prevent sticking.
Remove meat to warm platter.
Skim excess fat from pan juices.
Stir in ¼ cup sugar and 1 t Kitchen bouquet
Thicken juices with flour, if desired.
Makes 10-12 servings

BARBECUED FRANKS with CRANBERRY

12 franks	1½ t. white sauce
1 large onion	1½ t. dry mustard
3 T. butter	3 T. sugar
4 T. lemon juice	3 T. vinegar
½ c. celery	1 can cranberry
1 green pepper	sauce
¾ c. water	1 can tomato catsup

Chop onion, pepper and celery. Cook
slowly in butter until tender. Add
remaining ingredients and simmer
for 10 minutes.
Place franks in shallow baking dish
and cover with the sauce. Bake
at 350° for 30 minutes.
For a picnic, these rate A-1

CRANBERRY CHURCH PIE

Unflavored gelatin	1 T.
Cold water	½ C.
Cranberries	2 C.
Egg whites	2
Sugar	1 C.
Lemon juice	1 T.
Salt	¼ t.
Whipping Cream	1 C.
Sugar	1 T.

Prepare and bake 9" shell. Soften gelatin in water. Combine with CRANBERRIES. Bring to boil; simmer 5 mins. Stir often. Cool.

Combine egg whites, the 1 cup Sugar, lemon juice, salt and CRANBERRY mixture. Beat until firm peaks — about 6 to 8 mins. Pile into shell. Chill 4-5 hours. Whip cream and 1 T. sugar. Spoon atop pie.

CRANBROWNIES

1 15½ oz pkg. brownie mix — 2 T. corn syrup
1 8 oz can whole cranberry sauce. Ice Cream

Prepare fudge-like brownies. Cool slightly and cut into large squares. Blend cranberry and c. syrup. Top each square with a scoop of ice cream and then top each one with a spoonful of cranberry mixture.

HOT BUTTERED CRANGROG

1 32 oz cranberry juice cocktail
1 T. brown sugar - 2 inches cinnamon
½ t. each whole allspice and whole cloves
½ cup rum - Dash gr. nutmeg and salt
Butter or Margarine

Combine juice, sugar, spice and salt.
Slowly bring to a boil. Cover, simmer
for 20 minutes. Stir in rum and return
to boiling. Remove from heat. Place a
pat of butter in each mug. Pour in hot
rum mixture. (Makes 4 cups)

ACADIAN CRANBERRY - CHEESE BREAD

2 c. flour — 1 c. sugar — ½ t. soda
1½ t. baking powder — ½ t. salt
Juice of 1 orange — 2 t. grated orange peel
2 T. melted shortening — 1 egg, beaten
1½ c. shredded cheddar cheese (6 oz)
1 c. cranberries, halved
½ c. finely chopped walnuts

Mix berries with ¼ c. sugar and put aside.
Sift together dry ingredients, using the
¾ c. sugar. Combine orange juice
with water to make ¾ c. liquid. Add to
grated peel, melted shortening, cheese
and beaten egg. Pour into dry mixture.
Spread evenly in loaf pan. Bake in
moderate oven for 1 hour (350°).
Remove from pan. Cool. Best if
stored overnight.

DESSERT DEMONT

3 cups cranberry juice
2 3oz pkgs. strawberry gelatin
1 7oz. jar marshmallow creme
2 Tablespoons water
½ cup whipping cream, whipped
2 cups fresh or dry-pack frozen strawberries, halved.

Bring 2 cups juice to boil and dissolve gelatin. Stir in remaining cranberry juice. Chill slightly. Meanwhile, beat marshmallow creme and water at high speed Till mixture holds peaks. Fold in whipped cream.
Place gelatin in bowl of ice water and whip with electric mixer till fluffy. Fold marshmallow mixture and strawberries into gelatin.
Pour into 8-cup mold. Chill till firm. Unmold on serving plate.

CELERY CRANBERRY RELISH

1 lb. cranberries   -   2 cups chopped celery
1 unpared apple, cut -   1½ cups sugar
2 Tablespoons lemon juice

Chop - using coarse blade, cranberries, celery and apple. Stir in sugar and lemon juice. Cover and refrigerate.
MAKES ABOUT 4 CUPS.

91

CRANBERRY-APRICOT GLAZE

½ c. apricot preserves — dash ground cloves
1 c. finely chopped pecans
Roast last 30 minutes with glaze. Serve
remaining glaze over roast on serving
platter. Makes enough for a 5-lb. ham.

FORT ANNE CHICKEN

3 large chicken breasts
  (boned, skinned, halved lengthwise)
6 thin slices boiled ham
4 oz. Swiss cheese (6 3x½ inch sticks)
1 can whole cranberry sauce
¼ cup all-purpose flour
3 Tablespoons butter
⅓ cup sauterne
2 Tablespoons CORNSTARCH
2   "   COLD WATER
Toasted sliced almonds

Pound chicken lightly to make cutlets, ¼ inch.
Sprinkle with salt. Place ham slice, cheese
stick and T. cranberry sauce on each one.
Roll as for jelly roll. Coat with flour. Brown
in butter. Remove to 12x7x2 baking dish.
In same skillet, combine cranberry and
sauterne. Pour over chicken. Cover and
bake 1 hour at 350°. Remove to hot platter.

Combine CORNSTARCH and cold water. Add
pan juices and cook quickly, till thick.
Spoon some of sauce over chicken.
Top with almonds. Pass remaining
sauce. Makes 6 servings.

FRENCH PANCAKES

3 eggs, separated — ½ cup sifted flour
1 teaspoon sugar — 1 Tablespoon melted
½ "   salt   —   shortening
1 cup milk   — Cranberry Sauce (or Jelly)

Beat egg yolks and add sugar, salt and
½ cup milk. Add flour and shortening and
mix until smooth, then add the milk. Fold
in stiffly beaten egg whites. Bake on hot
griddle, making cakes larger than usual
and very thin. Spread with cranberry
mixture (sauce or jelly) and roll up while
hot. Serve with sprinkled confectioners'
sugar coating. Makes 12.

CRANAPPLE PANCAKES
Sift together:
2 cups flour   — ¼ cup sugar
4 teaspoons baking powder — 1 teaspoon salt
Combine 2 well-beaten egg yolks and
2 cups milk and add to dry mixture.
Stir in 2 Tablespoons melted butter
        1 cup chopped CRANBERRIES
        ½ cup finely chopped apple
Fold in 2 stiffly beaten egg whites
Let batter stand about 5 minutes.
Bake on hot griddle, using about ⅓ cup
batter for each. Serve with butter
and warm syrup. Makes 12.

PARKER'S COVE PUNCH

2 32 oz bottles cranberry
   juice cocktail
4 6 oz cans pink lemonade
   concentrate, thawed
6 cups cider or apple juice
12 inches cinnamon
2 t. whole cloves — 1 t. whole allspice
3 cups light rum

Be sure the 30-cup percolator is clean.
Combine juices and cider. Place spices
in coffee basket, place in percolator.
Plug in as for coffee. Then, after hot,
remove spices. Stir in rum and serve hot.

FIRE ISLAND PUNCH

1 fifth dry red wine — 3 whole cloves
2 cups cranberry juice cocktail
1 3x½-inch orange peel — 1 2x½-inch lemon peel
¼ c. sugar — ½ c. orange juice — ¼ c. rum
¼ c. lemon juice — ½ c. sugar cubes

Heat wine, juices, sugar, cloves, orange and
lemon peel. Do not boil. Pour into flame-
proof punch bowl. Place sugar cubes in
strainer; hold over punch. Heat rum.
Drizzle rum over cubes and ignite. As
flame rises, gradually spoon remaining
heated rum from a long-handled ladle
over cubes. When all sugar is melted
into punch, add orange slices for garnish.
Makes about 6 cups.

CRANAPPLE JAM

2 cups whole fresh cranberries
1 cup peeled, chopped Golden Delicious Apples
1½ cups sugar — 2 tsps. lemon peel (grated)
4 tsps. lemon juice — ½ tsp. butter

Crush berries and combine all
ingredients in 3 qt. saucepan. Cook
until mixture is thickened, stirring
often. Spoon into 1 pint container
and serve either warm or cold.
Store up to 1 month in refrigerator.
(45 calories per Tablespoon)

GRANVILLE MARMALADE

2 cups cranberries   2 lemons
2 grapefruit   2 oranges

Wash fruit. Slice citrus paper-thin.
Put seeds in small piece of cheesecloth.
Chop cranberries.

Measure fruit and add 2 cups water
for each cup of fruit. Stand uncovered
about 24 hours.

Remove seed bag. Cook over low heat
until berries are softened. Cool.

Measure fruit and add equal amount
of sugar. Cook slowly until thick. Pour
immediately into hot sterilized jars.

FRUITCAKE COOKIES

4 T. butter — 1 egg — ¾ c. brown sugar
¼ c. milk — 1 t. lemon juice — 1 c. flour
¼ t. each baking soda and salt — and gr. cloves
½ t. each ground cinnamon and allspice
1 c. chopped mixed candied fruits + peels
1 c. cranberries, chopped — Dash nutmeg
1 c. chopped nuts

Cream butter and sugar till fluffy; beat
in egg. Combine milk and lemon juice.
Gradually add to creamed mixture.
Stir in fruits and nuts. Drop by teaspoon
on lightly greased cookie sheet.
Bake at 375° for 10-12 mins. (Makes 4 dozen)

CRANBERRY-RASPBERRY MARBLE

Dissolve 1 small raspberry gelatin in
1 c. boiling water. Sieve 1-10oz. pkg. frozen
thawed raspberries. Add to gelatin with
1 cup cranberry sauce. Chill till partially
set.
Soften 1 envelope (1 T.) unflavored gelatin
in ⅔ c. cold water. Stir over low heat
until dissolved. Add 2 T. lemon juice. Cool.
Prepare 1 small pkg. dessert topping mix.
Beat in 2 small cream cheese and add to
unflavored gelatin. Chill till partially set.
Fold in 1 16oz can sliced peaches- drained
and diced.
Layer raspberry and peach mixture in a
7-cup mold. Swirl with spoon to marble.
Chill overnight. Serves 10.

SUNDAY SALAD   (Jellied)

2 envelopes unflavored gelatin — 1/3 c. sugar
1½ c. hot cranberry juice cocktail — ¼ t. salt
1/3 c. lemon juice — ¾ c. chopped celery
2½ c. cold cranberry juice cocktail
1½ c. chopped unpeeled apple — ½ c. walnuts
Dressing - (equal parts mayonnaise + sour cream)

Soften gelatin in ¾ cup
cold water. Add hot juice,
sugar and salt and stir
Till gelatin is dissolved.
Add lemon juice and cold
cranberry juice. Cool.
Put ¾ C. of mixture in
bottom of 2½ quart mold.
Chill till firm.
Chill remaining mixture till
it begins to set, then fold
in remaining ingredients,
except the dressing.
Put in mold and chill overnight. When
ready to serve, unmold, decorate with
lettuce or greens and top with dressing.

The cranberry is abundant, inexpensive,
rich in Vitamin C and Vitamin A, iodine
and calcium, can be stored in 'frig
or frozen and keeps its distinctive
color and flavour while stored or
frozen.

FROZEN CRAN-PINEAPPLE SALAD

Mix thoroughly 1 can drained crushed pineapple, 1½ c. cranberry sauce, 1 c. sour cream and ¼ c. chopped pecans. Put in refrigerator tray and freeze at least 3 hours. A half hour before serving, remove from freezer and place in refrigerator.

Cranberry juice cocktail and cranapple are produced in JAPAN by the soy sauce people, Kikkoman. They use the raw fruit from Ocean Spray but cannot use the familiar Trademark, because a whiskey manufacturer had already registered the word "ocean."

CRANPEAR COMPOTE

1 can cranberry sauce — ⅓ cup sugar
¼ teaspoon ground cinnamon — 1 T. lemon juice
¼   "   "   ginger
2 med. oranges, peeled and sliced
6 fresh pears, pared, cored & quartered

Combine sauce, sugar, juice, spices and bring to boil. Halve orange slices and place with pears in 1½ quart casserole or baking dish. Pour cranberry mixture over fruit. Cover and bake at 350° for about 40 minutes or till pears are tender. Spoon fruit mixture into sherbet glasses or compote. Serve warm.

BAKED CRANBERRY- WALNUT RELISH

1 lb. cranberries — 2½ c. sugar
1 c. walnuts, broken — 1 c. orange-marmalade
Juice of 1 lemon or lime —

Wash and drain berries. Stir in sugar, put in shallow dish and bake. Cover tightly, set oven at 350° for about one hour. Toast walnuts for last 10 minutes of baking. Add nuts and remaining ingredients to cranberries. Mix well and chill. Makes about 4 cups.

Stores in Tokyo, Osaka, Yokohama and Kobe sell cranberry products under a label called "CRANBY."

CRANBERRY BANANA

1 16 oz can jellied cranberry sauce
1 apple, pared & grated
2 bananas, mashed
⅓ cup Confectioners' sugar
1 t. vanilla - ¼ c. walnuts
1 cup whipped cream

Beat cranberry sauce till smooth. Stir in grated apple. Pour into 11x7x1½-inch pan. Fold bananas, sugar, vanilla and half the nuts into whipped cream. Spread over cranberry layer. Sprinkle with remaining nuts. Freeze till firm. Stand at room temp. 15 mins.
Cut in squares.

A well-known painting of the 1880s is called CRANBERRY HARVEST ON NANTUCKET. It is on display at Cranberry World in Plymouth, Mass. This newly opened tourist attraction is the home of Ocean Spray, Inc. Since the first can of sauce in 1920, Ocean Spray, Inc. has been known as the Cranberry King.

CRANBERRY ORANGE CHEESE MOLD

1 pkg. (6 oz) Orange (or raspberry) gelatin
1 cup boiling water — 2 cups ice water
1 cup finely chopped cranberries
Grated rind of two oranges
1 cup sour cream
1/4 cup chopped walnuts (optional)

Stir gelatin in boiling water till dissolved, then stir in water. Pour about 1/4 cup gelatin mixture into tall 5½ cup mold. Refrigerate till firm, about 20 minutes. (10 mins. in freezer). Arrange about 3 T. mixture cranberry and orange over molded gelatin. Refrigerate.
Fold sour cream into remaining gelatin mixture and chill. When thickened, fold in remaining cranberry-orange mixture and nuts. Spoon over firm gelatin in mold. Chill. Serves 8.

GRANVILLE JAM

Crush 2 cups cranberries, combine with:
1 cup apple (peeled, chopped)
1½ cups sugar ~ 4 t. lemon juice
2 t. lemon peel (grated) ~½ t. butter
Cook till thickened. Stir often.
Spoon into 1 pint container and serve
either warm or cold. Store up to
1 month in refrigerator.

There is a new cranberry liqueur
on the market, in a fancy bottle.
The liqueur is called - what else?-
Boggs' Cranberry Liqueur.

PUMPKIN SURPRISE
PIE

Spread ½ cup cranberry sauce in
bottom of 1 unbaked 9-inch shell.
Mix pumpkin (1½ cups) with ½ c. brown
sugar, 3 eggs, evaporated milk (1¼ cups),
2 teaspoons pumpkin pie spice, and ¼ t.
salt. Beat smooth. Pour over sauce
in shell. Bake 50 mins. (400°). Cool.

Garnish with whipped cream. Drizzle
with CRANBERRY SYRUP:
        Combine ¼ cup sugar
                1 T. cornstarch
                1 cup cranberry juice
        Cook and stir until thickens.
Add few drops red food coloring.
Cool. Makes about 1 cup syrup.

CRANBERRY APPLESAUCE (Freezer recipe)

Combine 6 apples, cored and sliced, with 1 cup cranberries and water. Bring to boil. Cover. Cook slowly till apples are tender — about 15 minutes.
Add: 2/3 c. sugar — 1/2 t. cinnamon
1 T. lemon juice
Cook until sugar is dissolved. Refrigerate.

To Freeze: Ladle into foil lined dish and put in freezer. Remove foil wrapped block, overwrap, seal. Label, date and return to freezer. Store up to 6 months. To serve, remove outer wrap and cook. Use hot oven - 400° - covered, about 35 mins.

CRANBERRY cultivation soon spread beyond New England.
1835 - New Jersey   1860 - Nova Scotia
1853 - Wisconsin   1883 - Washington
1885 - Oregon

MULLED CRANBERRY PUNCH

2 T. whole cloves — 1 T. whole allspice — 1/2 c. sugar
12 inches cinnamon, broken up — 5 cups water
2 1/2 cups grapefruit juice — 1/4 teaspoon salt
2 16 oz cans jellied cranberry sauce, mashed
Few drops red food coloring
Tie spices in cheesecloth. In large pan combine ingredients, slowly bring to boil. Simmer 5 mins. Remove spices. Serve warm with spice sticks. Makes about 10 mugs.

CRANBERRY BRACER

1 32 oz bottle low calorie chilled
       cranberry juice cocktail
1   6 oz can frozen orange juice
       concentrate, thawed
¼ teaspoon ground ginger
1   28 oz bottle carbonated water, chilled

Combine first three and chill.
Just before serving, slowly add
carbonated water. Stir gently.
Serve over ice in tall glasses.
Makes 8 tall glasses.

During the American Bicentennial year,
Seagrams advertised a new drink,
combining Seven Crown whiskey and
cranberry juice. It is called the
Firecracker.

CRANBERRY TOPPING

Blend 2 T. cornstarch with
½ c. water. Add 1 lb. cranberries, 1 c. sugar and
¾ t. cinnamon. Bring
to boil and cook, stirring,
until cranberries burst
and mixture thickens.
CRUMB TOPPING — Mix ¼ c. flour
and ⅓ c. packed brown sugar.
Cut in ¼ c. butter, softened, until
crumbly.

— CRANBERRY- ALMOND CRUNCH PIE —

1 8-oz pkg. creamed cheese
3 cups canned **cranberry sauce**
⅓ cup brown sugar
3 Tablespoons cornstarch
Dash of salt
⅓ cup sifted all-purpose flour
⅓ cup brown sugar
2 Tablespoons butter (margarine)
½ cup slivered almonds, ~~toasted~~

(1 - 9" - unbaked pastry shell)

Blend cream cheese with ½ cup of the
CRANBERRY SAUCE. Spread in pie shell.
Combine first ⅓ cup brown sugar,
cornstarch and salt. Blend remaining
CRANBERRY SAUCE. Spread carefully
over cheese layer. Bake for 35 mins.
in 375° oven.

Combine flour and rest of brown sugar.
Add butter until coarse crumbs.
Stir in almonds. Sprinkle over pie.
Bake 10-15 mins. more or until centre
of pie is firm. Serve warm or chilled.

Per capita consumption of cranberries
in Nova Scotia is about ½ lb. Total
consumption is about 375,000 lbs.
annually.

The cranberry is nearly round in shape and it measures up to 3/4ths of an inch when cultivated. The cranberry plant is an evergreen.

CRANBERRY-RAISIN CONSERVE

4 c. cranberries   2 c. sugar   1 c. water
1 lemon, seeded   1/2 c. raisins
1/2 c. slivered almonds

Combine all except almonds and boil 10 minutes. (Cut lemon into paper thin slices). Stir in almonds and pour into glasses. Cover, cool and refrigerate. Makes about 4 cups.
Variations: Substitute chopped prunes; Add 2 T. chopped crystallized ginger.

In Nova Scotia there are 7 cranberry producers. There are two cranberry farms in Ontario and one in Quebec.

CRANBERRY-HAM AND FRUIT MOLD

2 pkgs (3 oz) orange gelatin - 1 c. boiling water
2-1/2 c. cranberry juice cocktail
1 c. each peeled and diced peaches,
    melon and apple
2 c. diced smoked ham.
Dissolve gelatin. Stir in juice. Chill until syrupy. Fold in fruit and ham. Pour into 2 qt. mold. Chill till firm.
Serve with mayonnaise thinned with orange juice.

Double Nut/Fruit Bread

3 cups flour
1   "   sugar
4 t. baking powder
1 t. salt
1 beaten egg
1½ cups milk
2 T. cooking oil
1 cup cranberries - coarsely chopped
½ " mixed candied fruits and peels - chopped
½ " chopped walnuts and pecans

Sift together first four ingredients. Combine next three and add to dry mixture. Fold in CRANBERRIES, candied fruits and peels, and nuts. Pour into greased and floured pan - 9 x 5 x 3-inch. Bake 60-70 mins. (350°). Remove from pan.

Recorded production and consumption figures are misleading as they do not, and could not, include the many pails of berries picked off the wild cranberry bogs.

FROSTED CARDAMON BERRIES. Beat 1 egg white till foamy. Combine 1½ c. sugar and 1 t. ground cardamon. Coat 4 cups cranberries in egg. Toss in sugar mixture. Dry in shallow pan at room temperature. Store in airtight container up to 3 weeks - room temperature. Makes 4 cups.

The Indians mixed cranberries with beans and corn to make a sort of succotash.

CRANBERRY PIE

3½ c. cranberries   1½ c. sugar
1½ T. flour   ¼ t. salt
3 T. water   2 T. butter

Chop berries and mix all ingredients.
Fill pie shell (unbaked) and arrange
strips of crust criss-cross over top.
Bake at 450° 10 mins. Reduce to 350°
and bake 40 mins. longer.

Cranberries are borne on runners
called "uprights." Sometimes these
runners are 6' or more in length.

SPICED GRANVILLE WASSAIL

6 inches stick cinnamon, broken
16 whole cloves ⎯ 3 med. oranges
1 teaspoon whole allspice ⎯ whole cloves
6 cups cider or apple juice ⎯ ¼ c. sugar
1 16oz bottle cranberry juice cocktail
1 t. aromatic bitters ⎯ 1 cup rum

Tie cinnamon, 16 whole cloves and allspice
in a cheesecloth bag. Stud oranges with
additional cloves.
In saucepan, combine cider, cranberry,
sugar and bitters. Add spice bag and
oranges. Simmer, covered, 10 minutes.
Stir in rum and heat through.
Remove spices and oranges.
Pour into warm serving bowl.
Float oranges on top. Makes 9 cups.

Digby Gap and Annapolis Basin (St. George's Channel). From the Road to Annapolis.

Digby Sweet-Sour Pork

1½ lbs. boneless pork shoulder - small cubes
  1 T. cooking oil   1 T. cornstarch
  1 t. salt   ¼ cup cold water
  Dash of pepper   1 green pepper- strips
  1- 8¾ oz. can pineapple tidbits
  1- 8 oz. can (1 cup) CRANBERRY SAUCE
  ½ cup barbecue sauce
  Hot cooked rice

Brown meat in hot oil. Add salt + pepper.
Drain pineapple - save syrup. Add water
to make ¾ cup. Stir syrup, cranberry
sauce, + barbecue sauce into browned
meat. Cover and simmer 40-45 mins.
Blend cornstarch with cold water.
Stir into meat. Cook and stir until
mixture thickens. Add pineapple and
green pepper; heat through. Serve
over hot cooked rice. About 6 servings.

SPICY ICED TEA

2½ c. boiling water — ¾ cup sugar
5 Tea bags or 5 teaspoons loose tea
¼ teaspoon each ground nutmeg & cinnamon
2 cups cranberry juice cocktail
1½ cups water — ½ c. each orange
                          and lemon juice

Pour boiling water over tea and spices.
Steep 5 minutes. Remove tea and strain.
Add sugar and stir until dissolved. Cool.
Add remaining ingredients. Chill.
Serve over ice cubes in pitcher. (7cups)

Cranberries are now marketed
seriously in America, Canada,
the Pacific and in Europe. In
Scandinavia they are viewed as the
American version of lingonberries;
in Germany as preiselberries.

GRANVILLE CHICKEN - (curried)

2 large oranges — 2 bananas - Greens
4 cups cubed, cooked chicken — 1 t. curry
½ c. light raisins — ½ c. peanuts
1 c. jellied, cubed cranberry sauce
1 c. mayonnaise — ½ c. chopped chutney
2 T. orange juice

Section oranges, cut bananas diagonally
and dip in juice from oranges. Line
bowl with salad greens. Arrange all
except last three items and curry
and place on greens. Combine rest
for dressing.

— CRAN-HAM LOAF —

2 Eggs
3/4 C. Milk
1 teaspoon Salt
1/8 " Pepper
1 cup soft bread crumbs
1 pound each:
    Ground ham + Ground pork
Cranberry Sauce - 1 1/2 cups
1/8 teaspoon ground cloves

Beat eggs. Add milk, salt, pepper
and soft bread crumbs. Add meat.
Mix well.
Spread into loaf pan. Combine
CRANBERRY SAUCE and cloves.
Spread on top of loaf.

Bake 1 hour at 400° F.   Serves 8.

Among the Eastern Indians the
cranberry was called sassamenesh.

CRANBERRY DEBBIE — Dissolve 1 pkg. raspberry
gelatin and add 1/2 c. cold water. Cool. Put
2 c. cranberries and 1 orange through
chopper. Add 1 c. sugar and mix well.
When thickened, fold into the gelatin the
cranberry-orange mixture.
Pour into larger mold or individual
molds. Chill till firm.

110

HAWAIIAN PUNCH : Combine in a blender:
5 C. CRANAPPLE drink — ½ C. rum
2 T. lime juice — 1 T. sugar
1 4¾ oz jar strained banana baby food
Blend at high speed about 30 seconds.
Serve over ice rocks. Makes about
4½ cups.

Cranberry wine is becoming popular now
that cranberries are available year
round. Many bogs invite you to come
and pick-your-own ; the owners, that is.

CRANBERRIE- COTTAGE TUNA - (salad)
3 envelopes unflavored gelatin
2 cans (10½oz) cond. cream of mushroom soup
¼ c. mayonnaise — 1 T. parsley flakes
2 cans (6½ or 7oz) tuna - salad greens
¼ c. chopped walnuts — ¼ c. diced celery
1 can whole-cranberry sauce

Soften 2 envelopes gelatin in ½ c. cold
water. Heat about ¼ of soup, add
gelatin and stir until dissolved. Stir
into remaining soup and cool. Fold
in mayonnaise, parsley, tuna and walnuts.
Pour into 2 qt. rectangular glass dish
and chill till firm. Stir up cranberry.

Soften remaining gelatin in ¼ c. cold water.
Set in pan of boiling water and stir gently.
Mix with stirred cranberry sauce and stir
in celery. Put on top of tuna layer and
chill till firm. Cut in squares and serve
on greens.

111

CRANBERRY WASSAIL

2 c. cranberry juice
1 6oz can frozen orange
2 c. water — 1 T. sugar
¼ t. ground allspice
1 fifth sauterne
Few drops red food coloring

Combine juices, water, sugar and allspice.
Bring to simmer. Add sauterne and heat well
but do not boil. Stir in few drops coloring.
Garnish with orange slices.
Makes 8 cups

The largest producer of Cranberries
in America is in Kenosha, Wisconsin.

CRANBERRY DUMPLINGS

2 cups cranberries

1½ cups sugar	—	½ cup orange juice
2/3 " flour	—	1 t. baking powder
Pinch of salt	—	¼ c. sugar
¼ c. flaked coconut	—	2 egg yolks
2 T. milk	—	2 T. butter

Combine in 2 quart pan the cranberries,
the 1½ c. sugar, 1 c. water and orange
juice. Sift together dry ingredients
and stir in coconut. Combine egg yolks,
milk and butter. Stir into flour mixture
until blended.

Drop in 4 portions onto boiling cranberry
mixture. Simmer tightly covered about
20 minutes. Serve with light cream.

ANNAPOLIS PUNCH

1 3oz pkg. cherry gelatin - 1 c. boiling water
1 6oz can frozen lemonade or
          pineapple-orange concentrate
3 cups cold water
1 32oz bottle cranberry juice cocktail
1 28 oz bottle gingerale, chilled.
     Fruit flavored sherbet (optional)
Combine and pour over ice cubes in punch
bowl.
For an added festive touch, add scoops
of sherbet.

SAUSAGE STUFFING BALLS

A glamorous garnish when heaped
around the turkey - stuffing too!
1 lb. bulk pork sausage - ½ c. chopped celery
¼ c. chopped onion   - 1 well-beaten egg
1 8 oz. pkg. herb-seasoned stuffing mix
¾ c. chopped cranberries - ¼ c. butter
          1 cup chicken broth
Cook - in skillet - sausage, celery and
onion until meat is lightly browned and
vegetables tender. Spoon off fat.

Combine meat mixture and stuffing mix.
Stir in chopped cranberries, egg and
chicken broth. Mix well. Shape into
8 - 10 balls. Place in 15½ x 10½ x 1 inch
baking dish. Brush with melted butter.
Bake 30 mins. at 325°.
          Lovely to eat - lovely to look at.

EXOTIC RIBS

1 can jellied cranberry sauce
½ c. brown sugar - ⅓ c. catsup
1 clove minced garlic - 1 t. salt
2 T. vinegar - 2 T. soy sauce
1 t. gr. ginger - Dash pepper
4 pounds pork spareribs

Combine all except pork and mix well.
Rub ribs with salt and pepper, then grill
about 20 minutes over low coals. Brown
on both sides about 15 minutes more.
Brush well with sauce and broil about
30 minutes or till meat is tender. Brush
often. Makes about 2 cups sauce

Decorate with pizzazz!
String cranberries and drape
your favorite evergreen on the
lawn. Or attach berries to
the boughs with straight pins.

BARBECUED PORK LOIN

Tie together 2 boned pork loins -(about
5-6 lbs. total). Fat side should be out,
and tied at 1½ inch intervals. Balance on
spit, insert thermometer. Season with S+P.
Roast at 170° about 3 hours, with drip pan.
GLAZE: Combine ¼ c. creamy peanut butter
and ½ cup jellied cranberry sauce, mashed.
Brush mixture over pork when 170° and
continue cooking and brushing about
20 minutes. About 15 servings.

CRANBERRY CONSERVE

Combine 4 c. cranberries in 1c. water.
Boil about 5 minutes or till berries pop.
Add 1 T. grated orange peel
    2 c. peeled, diced apple
    1 c. "   " orange
    1/2 c. seedless raisins
    3 1/2 c. sugar
Boil gently, about 25 minutes. Stir often.
Remove and stir in 1/2 c. blanched almonds.
Makes 6 (6oz.) jars. (Use sterilized jars)

BAKED BEANS GRANVILLE

Remember the Saturday night suppers
in the old church hall?
    1 1/2 cups dry pea or Navy beans
    1 1/2 teaspoons salt
    2 cups cranberry J. cocktail
Combine with 2 cups water - bring to a
boil. Boil about 2 minutes. Remove and
stand covered about 1 hour. Then cover
and simmer 1 hour. Drain, keeping liquid.
Combine beans with:
1/3 c. chopped onion - 1/4 c. catsup
2 T. brown sugar   - 2 T. molasses
1 t. dry mustard   - 1/8 t. gr. ginger
Pour half the bean mixture into 2-quart
bean pot. Dot with half of 1/4 pound
sliced salt pork. Repeat layers. Add
1 1/2 cups reserved liquid. Cover and
bake in 300° oven about 5-7 hours.
Add liquid as needed.
HINT- 1 C. CRANBERRY SAUCE IS REALLY GREAT WHEN
ADDED TO 1 large tin baked beans. Bake 1 hour.

CRANBERRY PUMPKIN MUFFINS

Sift together 2 cups flour, ¾ cup sugar,
3 teaspoons baking powder, 1 teaspoon salt,
½ teaspoon each cinnamon and allspice.

Beat ⅓ cup cooking oil, 2 eggs and ¾ can
pumpkin until barely blended. Add to
dry mixture. Stir slightly. Fold in
2 cups cranberries, coarsely chopped.
Spoon into 18 paper-lined muffin cups.
Bake at 400° for 20-30 minutes. (18)

CRANBERRY- PINEAPPLE CHUTNEY

8 dried hot red peppers — 3 c. wh. vinegar
2 cans pineapple chunks — 2 c. br. sugar
2 cups diced cranberries — 2 t. salt
1 cup raisins — 2 T. chopped candied
3 cloves crushed garlic   ginger
1 cup blanched almonds

Soak peppers about 30 mins. in ¼ cup
cold water, then chop. (Drain and
remove seeds first)
Drain syrup from pineapple into pot.
Add peppers and all ingredients
except pineapple and almonds and
boil 10 minutes.
Add pineapple and simmer 45 minutes
or until thick.
Add almonds. Pour into hot sterilized
jars. Seal. Process in water bath
for 5 minutes. Makes 6 (½ pt.) jars.

CRANBERRY OATMEAL COOKIES

1 cup shortening — 1½ cups brown sugar
½ cup sour milk or buttermilk
1¾ cup sifted flour — 2 eggs
1 t. each baking soda and baking powder
1 t. each salt and cinnamon and nutmeg
3 cups quick-cooking rolled oats
1½ cups fresh cranberries, chopped
½ cup chopped walnuts

Cream shortening, sugar and eggs.
Stir in milk. Sift together dry items.
Stir into creamed mixture. Stir in
oats, berries and nuts. Drop
2-inches apart on greased cookie
sheet. Bake at 400° for 10 minutes.
(Makes 4½ dozen)

NEW ENGLAND SPECIAL

1 c. soft margarine — 1½ c. sugar — 4 eggs
1½ t. almond extract — 1 8oz cream cheese
2¼ c. cake + pastry flour — 1½ t. baking powder
½ c. drained chopped maraschino cherries
½ c. chopped cranberries (stand after
    chopping until well drained)
½ c. chopped pecans or walnuts
¼ c. finely chopped pecans
1½ c. sifted icing sugar — 2 T. milk

Cream well: cream cheese, margarine,
sugar, beaten eggs and almond extract.
Add 2 c. flour sifted with baking powder.
Combine remaining flour with cherries and
cranberries and ½ c. chopped nuts.
Fold into batter. Grease a 9" bundt;
sprinkle with ¼ c. finely chopped nuts.
Bake at 325° for 1½ hours. Cool 5 mins
and remove from pan. Glaze with
mixture of icing sugar and milk.
Garnish with finely chopped pecans.

Makes thoughtful gift. Can be baked
in various containers:
– 2 cups batter in each of 3 greased 1-lb.
coffee cans. Bake at 325° for 1 hour.

– 1 cup batter in each of 5 greased loaf
pans (6"x 3½"). Bake at 325° about 45 mins.

HALF-TIME SNACK

¼ cup sugar — ¾ teaspoon curry powder
½ teaspoon salt — ⅛ " ground ginger
¼ cup vinegar — 1 Tablespoon molasses
1 8oz can jellied cranberry sauce
¾ teaspoon worcestershire sauce
2 5½ oz pkgs. cocktail franks, halved

In saucepan, combine sugar, curry, salt, ginger, cranberry, vinegar, molasses, and worcestershire sauce. Bring to boil. Simmer 5 minutes. Add franks. Simmer 5 minutes longer. Makes 2⅓ cups.

CRANBERRY PARFAIT PIE

1 cup cranberry cocktail
1 3-oz pkg. lemon flavored gelatin
½ cup cold water — 3 T. lemon juice
1 pint vanilla ice cream
1 teaspoon grated lemon peel
1 16-oz can whole cranberry sauce

Prepare and bake pastry shell. Bring cranberry juice to boiling. Dissolve gelatin in hot juice. Add cold water and ice cream, by spoonful. Stir until melted. Chill till mounds when dropped from a spoon. (20-30 mins.) Stir lemon peel and lemon juice into cranberry sauce - then fold into gelatin mixture. Chill again - (20-30 mins.) Pile into cooled pastry shell. Garnish with whipped cream and additional cranberry sauce, if desired.

CRANBERRY FLUFF

4 c. cranberries — 1 t. vanilla extract
¼ c. quick-cooking farina — 1 c. sugar
Milk or light cream — (Extra sugar?)

Combine berries and sugar in 2 c. water
and bring to a boil. Reduce heat, and
simmer, covered, about 20 minutes.
Strain and force through a sieve. Add
water to make up 3 cups of mixture.
Put back in saucepan and bring to boil.
Gradually turn in the farina, then
simmer, and stir, about 5 minutes.
Add vanilla and cool slightly. Beat
at high speed until fluffy and light
pink in color. Serve as dessert or
breakfast dish with cream, and
sugar. Makes 6 servings.

Polka-Dot Muffins

1 c. cranberries, chopped
½ c. sugar — 1 beaten egg
1 teaspoon grated orange peel
¼ c. sugar — ½ c. orange juice
2 T. cooking oil
2 c. packaged biscuit mix
Mix cranberries, ½ c. sugar, orange peel.
Then combine in another bowl egg, sugar,
juice and oil. Add to biscuit mix. Stir
slightly. Fold in cranberry mixture.
Fill greased muffin pans, about ⅔ full.
Bake at 400° for 20-25 mins. Makes 18.

CRANBERRY BARBECUE GLAZE

(Glaze for 2 medium chickens)

Combine, then stir over low heat till smooth:

1 can jellied cranberry sauce
1/4 cup soy sauce — 1/2 c. brown sugar
2 T. lemon juice — 1 t. dry mustard
1 t. ground ginger — 1 crushed garlic
        — Dash of salt —

Rub chicken with salt and pepper and cook over grill or in oven. During last 30 minutes, brush often with glaze. (About 1 1/2 cups glaze.)

TOMATO ASPIC

2 envelopes unflavored gelatin
2 cups low-calorie cranberry juice
2 cups Tomato juice — 1 T. lemon juice
1 t. grated onion — 1/4 t. salt
Dash cloves + Nutmeg — 1/2 c. chopped celery
1/2 cup shredded carrot
Shredded cabbage and green pepper
Serve with a Diet Dressing.

In sauce pan soften gelatin in 1 cup of cranberry juice. Stir over low heat Till dissolved. Stir in remaining cranberry juice, tomato juice, lemon juice, spices, onion and salt. Chill till partially set. Fold in celery and carrots.
Pour into 5-cup mold. Chill Till firm. Unmold on platter and surround with shredded cabbage and green pepper. Pass diet dressing.

CRANBERRY-WINTER PIE

1 pint lemon sherbet
1 pound **cranberries**
2 cups sugar
1 cup water
3 egg whites
½ teaspoon vanilla
¼ " cream of tartar
6 Tablespoons sugar

Bake pastry shell and cool. Spread
sherbet in bottom. Freeze until solid.
Combine CRANBERRIES, sugar and
water. Boil and stir constantly.
Cook until berries are barely tender,
but still plump. Drain and chill.
Add to pie, over the sherbet.
Prepare Meringue before serving.
Beat egg whites with vanilla and
cream of tartar till soft peaks form.
Add sugar, beating until peaks form.
Remove pie from freezer. Spread
Meringue over berries, being careful
to seal edge.
Place pie on cutting board and bake
3-4 mins. —475° oven. Serve immediately.

CRANBERRY FLORENCE (PIE)

Combine in bowl 1¾ cups flour and dash salt. Cut in ⅓ cup shortening until mixture resembles small peas. Sprinkle with ⅓ cup ice water and quickly shape into ball. Wrap in waxed paper and chill. (PASTRY)

Combine and set aside:
1 jar (32 oz) mincemeat
Grated rind of 1 lemon
1 cup chopped cranberries

Line 9" pan with pastry. Trim edges and flute in pattern. Add mincemeat. Brush top (full or lattice) with egg-yolk beaten with 2 tsp. milk or cream. Bake at 425° 10 mins. Reduce to 550° and bake 25-30 mins. more. Sprinkle with 3 Tablespoons light rum and serve slightly warm.
Variation - serve with whipped cream, ice cream or liqueur.

Note: Pie can be made ahead. Bake and cool. Cover tightly and refrigerate up to 1 week. Before serving, sprinkle with rum and nuts and prepare to heat at 325° for 20 minutes.

CRANBERRY CHEESE CAKE

<u>CRUST</u>: Combine 1 c. flour, ¼ c. sugar, and 1 t. grated lemon peel. Add 1 sl. beaten egg yolk and ¼ t. vanilla. Mix well. Pat ⅓ of dough in 9" springform pan. Bake 8 mins (400°) or till golden. Butter sides of pan; attach to bottom. Pat remaining dough on sides of pan to about 1¾".

Filling:

　5 (8 m) pkgs. creamed cheese (soft)
　¾ t. grated lemon peel
　¼ t. vanilla　　　¼ t. salt
　1¾ c. sugar　　　1 c. (4 or 5) eggs
　3 T. flour　　　　2 egg yolks
　¼ c. whipping cream

Beat cream cheese, add lemon and vanilla. Mix sugar, flour and salt. Blend into cheese. Add eggs and yolks, one at a time, beating just enough to blend. Gently stir in cream. Turn into crust in pan. Bake 12 mins. (450°), then 55 mins. (300°). Remove. Cool ½ hour. Loosen sides of cheesecake from pan with spatula. Cool ½ hr. more. Remove sides of pan. Cool 2 hrs. longer.

Top with CRANBERRY TOPPING
　　　　(see page 103)

124

BAKED CRANBERRY / BANANA

3 bananas — 2 T. lemon juice — 2 T. brandy
½ t. cinnamon — 1 can cranberry sauce

Slice bananas in half lengthwise, then in thirds. Dip in lemon juice and place in 11 x 7 inch baking pan. Sprinkle bananas with cinnamon. Mix sauce with brandy and pour over bananas, and bake 15 mins. at 350°. Serve as dessert or pass with meat.

CRANBERRY STEAMED
PUDDING

2 cups cranberries, sliced
1 cup raisins - ½ c. nuts
½ cup snipped dates
1⅓ cups sifted flour
½ cup light molasses
2 teaspoons baking soda
¼ teaspoon salt
Top with HARD SAUCE

Mix berries, nuts and fruits. Add flour and stir. Combine molasses, soda, salt and ⅓ c. boiling water. Stir into fruit mixture. Pour into 6-cup mold. Cover tightly with foil and tie with string. Place on rack in deep kettle. Add boiling water 1" deep. Cover. Steam 1¼ hours, adding water if needed. Cool 10 minutes. Unmold. Serve warm with HARD SAUCE. Reheat pudding by wrapping securely in foil. Heat about 30 mins. at 300°.

SALAD DRESSING

Combine 1 8oz cream cheese and 1 cup dairy sour cream. Blend well. Stir in ¾ c. CRANBERRY-ORANGE (homemade is best). Chill at least 2 hours. Serve on fruit salad.

CRANBERRY CRUNCH

1 c. sugar	1 T. cornstarch
¼ t. salt	1 t. vanilla extract
½ c. raisins	2 c. cranberries
½ c. flour	1 c. uncooked oats
⅓ c. margarine	1 c. brown sugar
Vanilla ice cream	

Mix sugar, cornstarch, vanilla and salt, and ½ c. water. Stir in berries and raisins. Bring to boil over medium heat. Reduce heat and simmer. Set aside. Mix oats, sugar and flour. Cut in margarine until crumbly. Sprinkle half of mixture in greased 8" square pan. Spread with berry filling and top with remaining oatmeal mixture. Bake in moderate oven (350°) about 45 mins. Serve topped with ice cream.

CRANBERRY-APPLE DUMPLINGS

1½ pkgs. piecrust mix (9½ - 11 ozs.)
3 T. butter - 3 T. sugar - ½ c. raisins
¾ c. finely chopped cranberries (or 1 cup)
1 T. chopped walnuts — ¾ t. cinnamon
6 large baking apples (I like Northern Spy)
2 T. lemon juice - 1 orange peel, grated
1 egg yolk — whole cloves

Make pastry as directed.
Form into a flat 8-inch round. Wrap in
waxed paper and refrigerate.
In small bowl combine 3 T. butter, sugar,
raisins, walnuts and cinnamon. Blend
with fork.
Core apples with corer.
Pare apples and brush with lemon juice.
Using spoon, fill apple hollows with
above mixture to which is added the
cranberries and orange peel.
Preheat oven to 425°. Grease well a
shallow baking pan - 15½ x 10½ x 1.

Remove pastry from refrigerator and
prepare as described on next page.........

CRANBERRY- APPLE DUMPLINGS (continued)

Divide pastry evenly in sixths, using a
floured pastry cloth or floured surface.
Form each in a round ball. Flatten each,
then roll out from centre into an 8½" square.
Trim edges - use pastry wheel or decorate
edges. Save trimmings.
Place an apple in centre of each square.
Brush lightly with water. Bring each
corner of square to top of apple, pinch
edges of pastry together firmly and cover
apple completely. Reroll trimmings ¼" thick.
With knife, cut out 24 leaves, 1¾" long and
¾" wide. Brush one end of leaf with water.
Press leaves on top of dumplings. Put clove
in centre. Brush with yolk mixed with
1 T. butter. Bake, brushing once with juice.
In about 40 mins.- pastry browned and
apples tender - remove with spatula.
Serve warm, topped with HARD SAUCE.

These crusted stuffed apples are a
special Nova Scotian/New England treat.
They can be prepared ahead and
served with softened ice cream, or your
favorite sauce.

CRANBERRY JELLY

Firm, fresh, red berries make the best
jelly. Wash, sort and stem. Barely cover
berries with water. Boil slowly till berries
burst.

Put fruit and juice into jelly bag or several
layers of cheesecloth. Hang it over a
large bowl so juice can drip. Do not
squeeze the bag.

Add 3 cups sugar for every 4 cups
juice. Stir and bring to boil. Test
with metal spoon, flipping up boiling
syrup and letting it run off the edge.
When two drops form a sheet, the jelly
is ready and should be removed at once
from the stove. Longer boiling will
make stiff jelly.

Pour jelly into hot sterilized jars. Cover
until jelly is well set, then seal with
layer of hot, melted paraffin.

Cranberry juice is used for treatment
of kidney stone problems. Patients
do not develop sensitivity to the
cranberry juice and cost is minimal.

CRAN-PINEAPPLE BAKE

Put 4 cups CRANBERRIES in 8x8x2-inch
baking dish. Stir in one can (20½ oz)
pineapple chunks and 1½ cup sugar.
Bake in 350° oven for 1 hour.
Serve warm with ice cream. Serves 8.

Cranberry blossoms are a delicate pale pink color. They seem to cover the ground like a "dusting" of pink powder over the green vines. The cranberry blossoms in late June or early July.

CRANBERRY WAFFLES

1¾ cups sifted flour
¼ " sugar
2½ teaspoons baking powder
½ " salt
2 beaten egg yolks
1¼ cups milk
2 Tablespoons cooking oil
1 Cup CRANBERRIES, chopped
2 stiffly beaten egg whites
Cider Sauce (see page 130)

Sift together first four items. Combine next three. Add to dry mixture and mix well. Stir in berries. Fold in egg whites. Bake in hot waffle baker. (12)

Cider Sauce: Mix 1 cup brown sugar, 1 cup cider, 1 Tablespoon butter, ½ teaspoon lemon juice, ¼ teaspoon cinnamon and dash gr. nutmeg. Bring to boil. Cook 30 mins. Makes 1 cup. (Try adding 1c. Cranberry juice. Iti good!)

The early settlers made wine from blackberry, elderberry, mulberry, dandelion and cranberry. They made beer from spruce, apples and wild cherry.

The crisp, crimson cranberry was used by the Indians for food and dyes and they used it as a basis for a poultice for blood poisoning.

SPARKLING CRANBERRY PUNCH -

Beat 1 can jellied cranberry sauce till smooth. Stir in 3/4 c. orange juice and 1/4 c. lemon juice. Pour over ice cubes in punch bowl. Carefully add 1 large bottle (3½ cups) chilled ginger ale. Mix gently.
When serving, float thin orange and lime slices and maraschino cherries.
Makes 1½ quarts.

Cranberries grow on low vines in marshy places and are picked in the fall.

CRANBERRY CATSUP

1 lb. Onions		Ground cloves
4 lb. Cranberries		cinnamon
2 c. water	1 T. each	allspice
2 c. vinegar		salt
4 c. sugar		pepper

Peel onions and chop fine. Add berries and water and cook. Rub through a sieve. Add remaining ingredients and boil until thick, stirring occasionally. Pour into hot jars and seal. Makes 6 pints.
Serve as a relish.

CRANBERRY-CHERRY MIST

Dissolve 1 pkg. black cherry gelatin in
3/4 c. hot water. Stir in 1 can cranberry
sauce and 1/4 c. gingerale. Pour into a
1 1/2 cup mold and chill Till firm.
Garnish with sour cream mixed with a
dash of ground cinnamon.

No. American literature notes many
references to the cranberry. In
1864 the records show that Gen. Grant
ordered that cranberries would be
served to the soldiers at Tgiving.

FROSTY CRANBERRY LOAF

1 3oz pkg. cream cheese   - 1/4 c. sugar
1 cup whipping cream   - Dash salt
1 can cranberry sauce   - 1/4 t. almond ext.
1/2 inch-thick slices angel cake

Combine cheese, sugar and salt, and
beat till fluffy. Fold in whipped cream.
Break up cranberry with a spoon
and fold into cream mixture. Spoon
half this mixture over bottom loaf
pan (9x5x3 inch). Arrange cake
slices, in single layer, over mixture.
(it might be necessary to trim cake
to fit pan). Repeat cranberry and
angel cake layers once. Freeze firm,
about 8 hours or overnight. Cut
ribbon loaf in slices to serve.
Makes 8 servings.

CELERY SEED DRESSING

Combine: ½ c. jellied cranberry sauce
⅓ c. frozen orange concentrate
⅓ c. honey - ⅓ c. salad oil
1 teaspoon celery seed

Beat with rotary beater till thickened.
Serve over fresh fruits on lettuce-
lined plates.

The cranberry season was short and
marked the end of the harvest
season. It was the last time before
the snows when families and friends
came together to pick berries. In
Time it was a long remembered and
eagerly anticipated social event.

VALENTINE SALAD LOAF ♥

Blend 1 8-oz cream cheese with ⅓ cup
mayonnaise. Stir in ½ cup chopped celery
and 1 - 8¾ oz drained crushed pineapple.
Combine above with: ½ cup avacado
(diced) dash of salt and 1 t. lemon juice.
Stir gently and then fold in 1 cup wh.
cream. Tint pink with food coloring.
Cube ¾ can jellied cranberry sauce
and fold in.
Freeze in 9x5x3-inch loaf pan.
Garnish servings with remaining jellied
cranberry sauce.

CRANBURGUN SALAD

Dissolve 2 small pkgs. raspberry gelatin in
2 cups boiling water.
Stir in 1 can cranberry sauce, 1 can crushed
pineapple (8¾oz), and ½ cup burgundy.
Chill till partially set and then fold in
⅓ cup chopped walnuts. Pour into 6-cup
mold. Chill till firm. Later, fill center
of mold with fruit sections (1 orange,
1 grapefruit).
Serve with Cheese Fluff Dressing:
Prepare 1 pkg. dessert topping mix.
Beat in 1 8oz. cream cheese. Fold in
1 teaspoon grated orange peel.
Makes 10-12 servings.

It is said that an old-
fashioned cranberry
pie is an unforgettable
gourmet experience.
It used brown sugar,
molasses and was
baked in a deep dish
to save the juice.

FRUIT SALAD DRESSING

In small bowl, beat 1 can cranberry sauce
till smooth. Gradually beat in ¾ cup salad oil.
Blend in 3 tablespoons lemon juice and pinch
salt. Serve with fruit salads.

The first carload of cranberries shipped to Montreal from N.S. was in 1892.

ROSY PEAR PIE

½	cup butter	1	cup sugar
¼	" sugar	1	cup water
½	teaspoon salt	3	cups fresh
2	eggs yolks		CRANBERRIES
1½	cups sifted flour	1	can (16-oz)
¼	cup cornstarch		pear halves
½	cup whipping cream, whipped		

¼ cup chopped toasted almonds

Cream butter, ¼ c. sugar and salt, until fluffy. Beat in egg yolks, and add flour. Add ¼ cup finely chopped toasted almonds. Form into ball. With floured hands, line bottom and sides of a 10-inch pan. Chill 30 mins. Prick with fork. Bake 12-15 mins. (425°). Cool.

In saucepan, combine cornstarch and 1 cup sugar; add water and berries. Cook quickly, stirring constantly, till mixture thickens. Cool. Spread in cooled pastry shell. Arrange pear halves over top of cooled cranberry mixture. Chill. Garnish with whipped cream swirls.

Note: If pears are quite ripe, I often heat juice, spice and coloring and when it comes to boil, pour it over the pears in the casserole.

135

MOCK CHERRY PIE

1 c. cranberries
1 c. raisins
1 c. sugar
1 T. flour
¼ c. boiling water
⅛ tsp. salt — ¼ tsp. vanilla

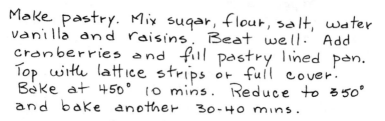

Make pastry. Mix sugar, flour, salt, water vanilla and raisins. Beat well. Add cranberries and fill pastry lined pan. Top with lattice strips or full cover. Bake at 450° 10 mins. Reduce to 350° and bake another 30-40 mins.

In winter, the frozen cranberry bogs made fine natural skating rinks.

CRANSALAD SOUFFLÉ

2 cups cranberry cocktail — 2 T. lemon juice
2 3oz pkgs. strawberry gelatin — 1 banana, sliced
1 16oz pkg. frozen strawberries, thawed
½ cup mayonnaise

Bring juice to boil, then stir in and dissolve gelatin. Drain strawberries, saving syrup. Add water to syrup to make 1 cup. Stir in gelatin mixture. Add lemon juice and mayonnaise. Beat with rotary beater to blend well.
Place in freezer till mixture is firm - about 30 minutes. Pour into mixer bowl and beat till fluffy. Fold in strawberries and bananas. Chill till firm in 8-cup mold.

Sand and water are two prerequisites
of proper cranberry cultivation.

Remolding Cranberry Sauce
Sometimes an opened can of jellied
cranberry sauce, needs a dress-up!
Lightly oil a 2-cup mold or individual
molds. Press sauce gently in molds.
Chill.

"..... by accident, I found that frozen
cranberries will blender chop much
more easily than trying to grind
fresh ones for my favorite cranberry relish." The Mirror, July '77.

CRANBERRY SALAD PARFAITS
    1   10 oz pkg. frozen raspberries
    1   "   "   "   blueberries
Partially thaw and drain, reserving ¼ cup
raspberry syrup.
Dressing: Blend together raspberry syrup,
          1 cup dairy sour cream and
          ½ teaspoon grated lemon peel.
{ 1 16oz carton creamed cottage cheese
{ 1 8oz can whole cranberry sauce
Spoon about 2 Table spoons cottage cheese
in each of 8 parfait glasses. Continue
layering with small amount of dressing,
raspberry, blueberry, cranberry. Repeat.
Serve immediately.

In Quebec there is a new cranberry
apéritif that is gaining reputation
across Canada.

Cranberry vinegar was a household pantry item in the late 1800s.

BASIC CRANBERRY PUNCH

BASE: 1 32oz CRANAPPLE DRINK, chilled, with
  ¼ c. lemon juice. (¼ c. grenadine optional).
With Spirit: Add 1 c. Vodka
With Soul: Slowly add to base, over ice in punch
  bowl, 1 28oz gingerale, chilled. Float scoops
  of raspberry sherbet (about 1 quart).
Wine: Add 1 fifth rosé wine, chilled.

The early settlers in Nova Scotia and New England made cranberry candles and cranberry soap.

CRANBERRY JUICE - with variations

① 4 c. cranberries — 4 c. water - ⅔ c. sugar
Cook until berries burst. Strain. Bring juice
to boil, then add sugar. Boil 2 mins.
Serve cold.

② ⎧ 9 lbs. cranberries - 9 quarts water
  ⎨ 2 T. whole cloves — 4 lbs. + 1 c. sugar
  ⎩ 1 c. lemon juice. Combine, cook and
strain berries, cloves and water. Add sugar
and stir. Chill. Add lemon juice before
serving. Makes 50 servings.

③ — 20 lbs. cranberries - 5 gals. water
    8½ lbs. sugar
Cook as in ① above

④ 1 gal. Cranberry Cocktail — 1 qt. gingerale
  1 48oz can Pineapple- Grapefruit juice
Combine well and serve over ice cubes.
  -OR- for the appropriate occasion, add:
    3 c. white rum and 1 c. peach brandy

Creeping Thistle

The cranberry is now being recognized as an under-utilized, relatively inexpensive food source.

SPICY CRANBERRIES
½ cup sugar — 1 cup water
2 inches cinnamon
1 cup cranberries

Combine sugar and half of water. Add spice and cook to boil, stirring often. Add berries and boil rapidly. Remove from heat when berries pop—about 2 minutes. Chill. Remove spice.

It takes 5-6 yrs. to bring a cranberry bog into production. The cost was about $5000 an acre in 1975. There are no nurseries in the cranberry business and new hybrids are scarce and expensive.

CRANBERRY-GRAPEFRUIT RELISH
2 c. cranberries — 1 grapefruit
¾ c. sugar.

Put berries through chopper. Add sugar and mix well. Peel, section and dice grapefruit. Stir into cranberries. Chill. Makes 2 cups.

The old Latin name "oxycoccus" means "sour berry."

MERRIE CRANBERRIE

Combine and serve in festive glasses:
- 3/4 cup cranberry cocktail
- 1 jigger bourbon

Serve over ice cubes.

The cranberry had a distinct and delightful effect on the education of young people. Schools did not reopen until October, after the peak of the cranberry pickin'.

MARITIME CHICKEN

Cover a 3-lb. ready-to-cook broiler-fryer cut up chicken with 1/2 cup flour and dash of salt. Brown in about 4 T. butter, turning once. Meanwhile, combine the following ingredients in a saucepan.

- 1 1/2 c. cranberries
- 1/4 c. chopped onion
- 1 t. grated orange peel
- 1/4 t. each of ginger and cinnamon
- 3/4 c. sugar
- 3/4 c. orange juice

Bring to boil and pour over chicken. Cover and cook slowly about 40 mins.

Cranberry juice is prescribed as a treatment of urinary tract infections where conventional antibiotics fail.

CRANPORT SALAD

Dissolve 2 small pkgs. raspberry gelatin in 2 cups boiling water. Stir in 1 16-oz can cranberry sauce and 1 8¾-oz can undrained crushed pineapple. Fold in ¼ cup chopped walnuts and add ¾ cup port. Pour into 6½ cup mold. Chill to firm.

Cranberry business outside the U.S. has tripled and it would seem that barely a dent has been made in the potential market.

CRANBERRY MOLDED RELISH

Dissolve small pkg. lemon and cherry gelatin in 3 cups boiling water, adding ½ cup sugar. Add 1 Tablespoon lemon juice and 1-8¾oz can undrained crushed pineapple. Chill till partially set.

Put 2 cups CRANBERRIES and 1 small orange, quartered and seeded, through grinder. Fold into gelatin mixture along with celery and nuts. Pour into 8½-cup mold. Chill till firm. Unmold on lettuce leaves.

The chemical properties in the cranberry make it an effective healer of diaper rash. Maybe one day it will appear on the market as a red powder!

Cranberry vines resemble strawberry plants. They each grow rapidly, with runners in all directions

CRANBERRY SWIRL CAKE

Make your favorite layer cake. After filling layer pans, with fork break up 1 c. cranberry sauce. Sprinkle over batter, with broad side of small spatula make zigzag strokes through batter (about 2 up and down strokes). Bake. Cool as desired. Ice with Cranberry Lemon Frosting.

The first cranberry cultivation in Canada was by Wm MacNeil of Melvern Square in Annapolis County of Nova Scotia.

CRANBERRY-PECAN TASSIES

Blend 1 3oz cream cheese and ½ c. butter. Stir in 1 c. flour and chill one hour. Shape into 2-dozen 1-inch balls. Place in ungreased muffin pan - about 1¾-inch cups. Press dough evenly against bottom and sides. Beat together:
   1 egg — ¾ c. br. sugar — 1 T. butter - vanilla
Stir in ⅓ c. finely chopped cranberries and 2 T. coarsely broken pecans.
Spoon into pastry lined muffin cups. Bake at 325° for about a half hour or Till filling is set. Cool in pans. Makes 24.

CRANBERRY KRISTIN - PIE

1½ c. finely crushed gingersnaps
2 T. sugar — ¼ c. softened butter
1 can cranberry sauce — ⅛ t. salt
1 cup raisins — 1 T. cornstarch
¼ t. nutmeg — 1 cup heavy cream
2 T. orange juice — 1 T. lemon juice
1 T. grated orange rind.

Mix gingersnaps and sugar. Add butter
and blend with fingers. Line greased
9" piepan with crumb mixture, pressing
well against sides.
Bake at 350° for 10 minutes. Cool.
Mix sauce, raisins, cornstarch, nutmeg
and salt and cook until clear and
slightly thickened. Cool.
Whip cream and fold into cranberry
mixture with remaining ingredients.
Pour into pie shell and chill.

Cranberry pickers wore large straw
hats or bonnets, a canvas apron,
knee patches and sturdy cotton
gloves. They used a wooden hand
scoop now found only in antique
shops or old sheds or attics.

Four Fruit CHUTNEY

3 lbs. firm ripe Bartlett pears
2 cups chopped cranberries
1 can ea. cherry & peach pie filling
1 cup brown sugar — 1 T. garlic salt
3 t. granulated sugar — 3/4 c. cider vinegar

Halve, core and dice pears. Measure
9 cups. Add remaining ingredients
in large kettle and simmer, uncovered,
about 1 hour. Pour into 10 hot jars
(1/2 pt.) and seal. Process in water
bath for 5 minutes.

Cranberry pickin' time meant a series
of picnics - boiled eggs, homemade
bread and doughnuts. It was a
fine chance for the young men to
entertain with their feats of daring.

CRANBERRY CHUTNEY

4 cups cranberries
1 apple - tart, pared, cored, diced
2 cups brown sugar
3/4 " vinegar
1/2 " chopped mixed candied fruits
1/2 teaspoon salt   and peels
1/4 " ginger, cloves, allspice, mustard (ea.)

Combine above in 3-qt. pan. Boil, then
simmer, uncovered, 15 minutes, stirring
occasionally. Cool. Refrigerate or freeze
in airtight containers. Makes 4 1/2 cups.

CRANBERRY SURPRISE

Wash, dry and grease sides and bottoms of 6 frozen juice cans. Preheat oven 375°. Prepare 1 pkg. orange muffin mix. Fold in 1 c. finely chopped nuts and 3/4 c. cranberry sauce. Spoon into greased cans, filling 2/3 full. Bake 35 mins. Cool. Ease out with spatula. Cool, slice. Wrap in foil for very thin slices. Keep a couple days before using or freeze. Slices can be cubed for garnish and for tossed salads.

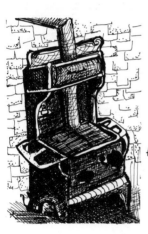

CHRISTMAS CARROT CAKE

Sift together:
1 1/2 c. flour
1 t. each baking powder
        and " soda
1/2 t. salt
1/2 t. each nutmeg + cinnamon
Add to dry mixture:
1 c. shredded carrots
1/2 c. cranberry sauce
1 c. sugar
2/3 c. cooking oil
2 eggs.

Beat until well blended. Pour into greased and floured 9x9x2-inch dish. Bake 350° - 40-45 minutes. Combine 1/2 c. sifted Confectioners' sugar and 1 Tablespoon light cream. Drizzle over the cake. Variation: bake in 2-qt. mold!

CRANBERRIE COTTAGE PORK ROAST

5½ - 6 lb. Crown roast of pork. (12-16 ribs)
Place roast in shallow pan, bone ends
down. Roast in 325° oven till 170° by
inserted thermometer. or about 3½ hours.
Combine ½ c. CRANBERRY JUICE COCKTAIL
and 2 T. light corn syrup and baste
roast 4 times during last oven hour.

In saucepan, combine 1 cup cranberry
sauce, ½ cup apricot preserves, ¼ cup
cranberry juice, ¼ t. each salt + cinnamon.
Bring to a boil.
In a 2-quart casserole, place 2 cans
drained sweet potatoes. Pour half the
sauce over potatoes. Cover and bake
along with roast the last 45 minutes.
To serve, place roast on warm platter.
Arrange sweet potatoes in "crown"
center and around roast. Spoon
remaining half of sauce on potatoes.

GRAVY: Skim fat from pan juice. Add
water to make 2 cups. Add 2 T. cornstarch
and 2 T. cold water. Cook quickly till thick.
Pass gravy with meat.
Slice between ribs. About 12-16 servings.

Honey and Poppy seed Dressing.

Combine ¼ c. honey, 3 T. lemon juice,
2 T. oil and 2 t. poppy seed. Chill
several hours to blend flavors.

CRANBERRY SQUASH

4 small acorn squash - ½ c. brown sugar
1 cup chopped unpared apple - 2 T. butter
1 cup chopped cranberries
1 orange, peeled and diced

Cut squash in half length wise and remove seeds. Place cut side down in 13x9x2-inch pan. Bake 35 mins. in 350° oven. Turn cut side up and sprinkle with salt. Combine rest of ingredients and fill squash with the mixture. Continue baking 25 mins. or till squash is tender. 8 servings.

HAM WITH RAISIN SAUCE

1 5 lb. canned ham — 1 10 oz. apple jelly
1 T. prepared mustard — ¼ c. dry wh. wine
⅓ c. cranberry juice — ½ c. light raisins
1 can whole cranberry sauce

Bake ham as directed on can. Then combine jelly and mustard. Stir in wine and cranberry juice. Cook and stir to boiling. Simmer 3 minutes. During last 30 mins. in oven, pour ⅓ of glaze over ham and repeat every half hour.*
In saucepan, bring cranberry sauce and raisins to boil. Remove ham to warm platter. Add glaze from pan to cranberry mixture; bring to boil. Spoon over ham. Pass remainder.
Makes 2½ cups sauce.
Makes about 15 servings of ham.

*Sometimes I baste with glaze every 10 mins.

GRANVILLE SHERBET

Soften 1 envelope of
gelatin in ½ c. water.
Combine:
  1 lb. cranberries
  2 c. sugar
  ½ c. orange juice
Cook until berries burst. Add gelatin and
stir until dissolved. Remove and cool.
Whirl in blender until smooth. Add
1½ c. light cream. Mix well.
Pour into refrigerator trays. Freeze.
Cover to store.

CRANBERRY PEACH PIE

1 can (29 oz) peach slices
3 cups CRANBERRIES
1½ " sugar - 3 T. cornstarch
¼ " chopped toasted almonds
Pastry for 2-crust lattice-top pie.

Drain peaches, keeping 1 c. syrup.
Cut up peaches and set aside.
Combine cranberries and syrup.
Cook till berries burst. (You may wish
to remove some berries for garnish).

Combine sugar and cornstarch. Add to
hot cranberries. Cook quickly. Remove.
Stir in peaches and almonds. Turn into
9-inch pie plate, pastry lined. Add
lattice top. Seal and crimp edges.
Bake 35-40 mins. (400°).

BURGUNDY PUNCH - (makes about 7 cups)

3/4 cup sugar - 6 inches stick cinnamon
1 teaspoon whole cloves — 2 cups burgundy
1 32 oz bottle cranberry-apple drink

Combine and boil 1 minute, all except
wine and juice. Strain out spices
and chill. Combine with chilled
wine and cranberry-apple drink.

CAPE COD JAM
(Cranberry and Gooseberry)

3/4 lb. gooseberries — 1/2 lb. cranberries
3 c. sugar — 1/2 lb. cooking apples — 1 lemon

Remove cases from gooseberries before
weighing. Put fruit in large saucepan
and crush with potato masher.
Sprinkle half of sugar over the fruit.
Cover and stand overnight to draw out
the juice. Next day add peeled, cored,
finely chopped apple and bring to boil.
Add remaining sugar and juice of the
lemon and boil steadily until jam will
set when tested.
Pour into warm dry jars and seal when
cooled.

This recipe makes
a splendid gift.

CRANBERRY BREADS

CRANBERRY ICE

1 qt. water — 3 c. sugar
1 qt. cranberries

Boil sugar and water together for 5 minutes. Boil cranberries in small amt. of water until soft, then press through a sieve. Add to syrup, cool and freeze.

CRANBERRY-ORANGE QUENCHER

Combine 1 32 oz bottle cranberry cocktail
with   1 cup orange juice and
         1 teaspoon mace.

Place an orange peel twist in each section of ice cube tray. Half fill each section with juice mixture. Freeze. Refrigerate rest of mixture.

One half hour before serving:
Remove tray from freezer. Thaw slightly. Put 2 or 3 cubes in each of 6 old-fashioned glasses. Pour refrigerated juice over ice cubes. Mixture will become slushy. Serve with teaspoons. Makes 6 (8 oz.) servings.

ORANGE-PEEL TWISTS

Slice oranges crosswise in thin slices. Cut each orange slice from edge to centre.
Twist each slice in opposite directions so slice will be perky.

Lemon-peel twists can be made in same way.

HOLIDAY JENNIFER (salad)

Blend 1 lb. cranberry sauce with 1 can
crushed pineapple and 2c. sugar.
Mix well. Let stand for 2 hours.
Add 1/4 lb. of marshmallows,
cut in small pieces.
Add 1/2 pt. whipped cream.
Mix well and serve.

This is a traditional dish from
the old homestead in Saskatchewan.

YOLANDE PARFAIT
(with cranberry + strawberry)

4 c. strawberries   2 c. cranberries
6 t. sugar   1/4 c. water
1 envelope unflavored gelatin
(artificial sweetener to equal 6t. sugar
   can be used for weight watchers)-
Pkg. Whipped Topping mix

Place berries in blender and blend
until chopped. Stir in sugar (or sweetener)
and set aside. In small saucepan
sprinkle gelatin over water and cook
over low heat until dissolved. Stir
in berry mixture. Divide into eight
parfait glasses alternating with
whipped Topping (check recipe) and
ending with whipped Topping.
Chill. (50 calories each with sweetener)

151

CRANBERRY-RICE DAINTY

1 c. cooked rice — 1 c. heavy cream
1 can. cranberry sauce
½ c. Confectioner's sugar

Chill rice and sauce. Mix rice and 1 c.
sauce. Add sugar and fold in whipped
cream. Pile in individual serving
dishes. Top with generous spoonful
of remaining cranberry sauce.

CRANBERRY EGGNOG PIE

1 baked 9-inch pastry shell
2 envelopes unflavored gelatin
3 cups dairy eggnog
1 cup whipping cream
1 can (16-oz) jellied cranberry sauce
   (chilled and cubed)

Soften gelatin in 1½ cups eggnog. Stir
over low heat until dissolved. Stir in
remaining eggnog. Chill till slightly
thickened; beat smooth. Whip ½ cup
of cream; fold into gelatin mixture.
Fold in 1½ cups cranberry cubes.
Pile into cooled shell. Chill.

Whip remaining cream; pile atop
chilled pie. Trim with rest of
jellied cranberry cubes.

CRANBERRY CHRISTINE
(layered salad)

This salad has three layers, each of which can be started simultaneously.

Bottom layer: Dissolve small pkg. lime gelatin in 1 c. boiling water. Drain 1-8oz can grapefruit, reserving syrup. Add water to make ¾ cup. Add to gelatin. Partially chill. Dice half an apple. Fold fruits into gelatin.

Middle layer: Dissolve small pkg. lemon gelatin in 1¼ c. boiling water. Stir in ¼c. lemon juice. Gradually add 1 8oz cream cheese. Beat smooth with electric beater. Partially chill. Top with 1 diced apple and ½ c. cashew nuts, folding barely into mixture. Chill.

Top layer: Dissolve strawberry gelatin in 1 c. boiling water. Stir in 1 16-oz can cranberry sauce. Partially chill. Core and halve 1 apple. Rub surface with lemon. Cut in slices and arrange around bottom of the mold. Fold ½ c. diced celery into gelatin and spoon over the apple.

Directions are given for salad as served. When making, begin with Top layer, as that is bottom layer in 8-cup mold.

Garnish with Frosted Cranberries.
 (see page 106)

QUICK and QUAINT with CRANBERRIES

SLOPPY JOES

1 lb. ground beef   -   1 cup chopped onion
1 cup chopped celery - ¼ t. chili powder
1 10 ¾ oz can condensed tomato soup
1 8 oz can (1 cup) whole cranberry sauce
Dash of salt   - Dash of bottled hot pepper sauce
8 hamburger buns, split and toasted

Brown the beef, adding onion and celery. Cook till tender but do not brown. Add tomato soup, cranberry sauce, salt, chili powder, and hot pepper sauce. Simmer about a half hour - uncovered. Spoon into toasted split buns.

TWO WHOLE-CRANBERRY SAUCES

    4 C.   CRANBERRIES
    2 c.   sugar
    2 T   minced crystallized ginger
         or
½ t ground ginger
Grated rind of 1 orange

Boil CRANBERRIES with ½ C water. Simmer 10 mins. or until berries pop. Pour into mixing bowl. Add sugar and stir until cool. Divide in half. Flavor one part with ginger and other part with orange rind. Store covered in refrigerator. About 1½ C each.

SPICY CRANBERRY CHEESE
SALAD MOLD

Dissolve 1 3oz orange-pineapple
gelatin in 1 cup boiling water;
add 1 cup orange juice. Chill.
Blend 1 small cream cheese into
½ cup whipped cream.
Add ¼ cup chopped pecans.
Fold into chilled gelatin mixture.
Pour into 9x9x2-inch dish. Chill.

Soften 1 envelope unflavored gelatin
in cold (¼ cup) water; dissolve over hot
water. Combine:
   1 can cranberry sauce
   2 T. lemon juice
   ¼ t. ground allspice
   ⅛ t. ground nutmeg
   1 cup orange sections
   1 cup ginger ale
Stir in softened gelatin. Pour over cream
cheese layer. Chill 4 to 5 hours, or
until firm. Serve in squares.
Variation: Omit orange sections from
mixture and use to top squares.

IRENE SUPREME - (Turkey salad open sandwich)
Combine and mix well:
2 c. diced cooked turkey — 1 c. cranberries
½ c. sliced celery — ¼ c. onion bits
1 c. pineapple chunks — 1 t. salt
2 t. lemon juice
Salad dressing to moisten.

Spread on 6 slices of toast. Top with
thin layer grated cheddar cheese.
Broil till cheese melts.

CRANBERRY STE CROIX
(frozen pie)

1¼ cups fine vanilla wafers   1 c. whipping cream
6 T. butter (melted)   ¼ c. sugar
1 8 oz. cream cheese   ½ t. vanilla
        1 16-oz. can cranberry sauce

Combine crumbs with melted butter.
Firmly line buttered 9-inch pie plate.
Chill till firm.
Beat cream cheese till fluffy. Combine
whipping cream, sugar and vanilla. Whip
until thickened - not stiff. Gradually add
to whipped cream cheese. Beat till smooth.

Save a few whole cranberries for garnish.
Fold CRANBERRY sauce into whipped mixture.
Spoon into chilled crust; freeze firm.
Remove 10 mins. before serving. Top with
additional whipped cream and garnish.

Bonus: A freezer make-ahead.

CRANBERRY-BREAD STUFFING

8 cups toasted bread pieces
1   "   salad dressing
1   "   finely chopped onion
⅔   "   thinly sliced celery
1   "   chopped cranberries
⅔   "   cold water
2 t. salt ~ 1 t. sage ~ 2 t. summer savory

Combine and mix lightly until well blended. Stuff Turkey or chicken or pork, or bake in a shallow greased pan at 550° for about 30 mins.

Allow about ¾ cup stuffing per pound.

CRANBERRY MEAT SAUCE

In large kettle, combine:
 4 quarts fresh cranberries, 2 c. onion-
 finely chopped, and 2 c. water.
Bring to boil, then cover and simmer 10mins.
Puree the mixture.
In kettle combine:
   Cranberry puree - 2 c. white sugar (or 4)
   2 c. white vinegar - 1 T. salt - 1 t. pepper
   1 T. each cloves, cinnamon, all spice, celery seed.
Bring to boil; simmer uncovered, 15-20 mins.
Stir to prevent sticking.
Remove and skim off foam. Ladle into hot jars, leaving a ½-inch space. Process in hot bath 5mins. after water boils. Serve with wild game or other meats. About 4 pints.

Muffin Surprise

1¾ c. flour — ¼ c. sugar — ¾ t. salt
2½ t. baking powder — 1 well beaten egg
¾ c. milk — ⅓ c. cooking oil (or shortening)
1 can jellied cranberry, cubed (½ inch).
Sift dry ingredients together. Combine
egg, milk and oil and add to dry mixture.
Fill greased muffin pans ⅓ full. Sprinkle
cranberry cubes over batter, then
cover with remaining batter. Bake at
400° for 25 minutes. Makes 12.

CROWN MERINGUE

3 egg whites — 1 t. vanilla — 1 c. sugar — salt
¼ t. cream of tartar — 1½ - 2 qts. ice cream
CRANBERRY SYRUP (see page 101)
Combine egg whites, vanilla, cream of tartar
and dash of salt. Beat till frothy. Gradually
add sugar, beating till stiff peaks form.
Cover baking dish with foil or ungreased
paper. Using 9" pan as guide, draw circle.
Spread meringue over circle, shaping into
shell with back of spoon. Bake at 275°
for 1 hour. Let dry in closed oven 2 hours.
Meanwhile, dip ice cream balls onto
baking sheet and place in freezer. Just
before serving, fill meringue with ice
cream balls and drizzle with
Cranberry Sauce. Serves 8-10.

APRICOT AUTUMN MOLD

Drain 1 30oz can apricot halves, saving syrup. Combine syrup, 2 T. vinegar, 7 cloves, 4 inches stick cinnamon and boil. Simmer 10 minutes. Strain and measure syrup. Add boiling water to make 2 cups. Pour over 1 3oz orange gelatin. Dissolve. Chill till partially set. Arrange apricots in 8, ½ cup molds. Cover with gelatin mixture. Chill firm. Unmold on cranberry slices (jellied sauce cut in slices)

SWEET N' SAUCY SPARERIBS

Cut 4 pounds spareribs in 2-inch wide pieces. Cover both sides with a mixture of: ⅛ t. garlic powder, ⅓ cup flour — 1½ teaspoons salt — ⅓ cup soy sauce Heat ⅓ cup cooking oil in 12-inch skillet and brown meaty parts of ribs, a few at a time. Drain. Combine with meat, cover and simmer 1½ hours:
½ cup vinegar — ½ cup cranberry juice
⅓ cup sugar — ¼ teaspoon ginger
Add 2 green peppers, cut in 1-inch squares. Cook 5 minutes. Remove ribs to hot platter.

Sauce:
Blend 2 teaspoons cornstarch with 1 T. cold water. Stir into pan juice and add ½ cup cranberry sauce. Cook but stir constantly, till mixture thickens.
Add 1 11oz can Mandarin oranges, in segments. Heat through.
Serve sauce over ribs and hot cooked rice. Makes 6 servings.

CRANBERRY MELON

Drain and reserve syrup from
  1 10 oz. pkg. frozen raspberries, thawed
Blend 2 T. syrup with 2 T. cornstarch. Set
aside. Combine remaining syrup,
½ c. currant jelly and ½ can cranberry
sauce. Sieve raspberries into mixture.
Cook quickly, stirring constantly, till thick.
Cool.
Quarter and seed 2 cantaloupe or
honeydew melons. Place scoop of
sherbet in center. Spoon cranberry-
raspberry sauce on top.
Makes 1⅔ cups sauce; Makes 8 servings.

SALAD JEANIE

1 pkg. (6 oz) lemon gelatin — 2 t. salt
¾ c. thin ham strips → ¾ c. thin process cheese
½ c. shredded lettuce → dash pepper strips.
¼ c. finely sliced onion → 2 c. boiling water
1 small tomato, wedged → 1 c. cold water
3 T. vinegar - ⅛ t. red pepper sauce
½ small green pepper, cut in thin strips
1 cup finely chopped cranberries

Dissolve gelatin and salt in
boiling water. Add cold water,
vinegar and pepper sauce.
Chill till thickened. Fold in
remaining ingredients. Pour
into 6-cup mold. Chill
at least six hours. Garnish
as desired.   6 servings.

The Puritans believed that "all things come from God" and so they reached out to the natural harvest around them.

CRANBERRY STEAK SUPREME

4 beef sirloin strip steaks, ½ inch thick
Pound with mallet. Spread one side with salt, freshly ground black pepper and dry mustard. Pound into meat. Repeat with other side of meat. Melt 2 T. butter in blazer pan of chafing dish over direct flame, or in skillet. Cook 2 steaks at a time, transferring to hot platter.
In blazer pan or skillet, combine
        ½ cup whole cranberry sauce
        ¼ cup dry red wine
1 t. Worcestershire sauce — 2 t. chives
Bring to boil. Return meat to chafing dish. Spoon sauce over meat. Garnish with 4 fresh mushroom crowns.

The social history of the cranberry opens many doors to the past, showing the links between the early days of the 13 colonies and the development of N.S. Seldom do we think of the role of the humble cranberry in the culture and economy of the past.

The first big frost marked the end of the regular harvest and the start of the "red gold" harvest.

SPICED GRANVILLE TEA

Combine 1 32oz bottle cranberry cocktail with 1 3" cinnamon stick and ½t. whole cloves. Secure top and refrigerate.
To serve hot, put mixture in pan with 1qt. water, ⅓ c. honey and 1 T. lemon-flavored Instant Tea.
Heat and serve in mugs with lemon slice floating on top. About 8 mugs.

Early experimentation with cranberry plants followed the observation that the biggest fruit grew where shore sand drifted in and out of the vines.

CRANBERRY MUFFINS

¾ c. cranberries ⌣ ½ c. powdered sugar
2 c. flour ⌣ 3 tsp. baking powder
½ t. salt ⌣ 4 T. sugar ⌣ 1 beaten egg
1 c. milk ⌣ 4 T. melted shortening

(Half of batter can be frozen for later). Chop cranberries once and mix with powdered sugar. Let stand while sifting dry ingredients. Add egg, milk and shortening. Then add sugared cranberries. Mix but do not beat. Bake at 350° for 20 minutes. (Makes 12)

CRANBERRY MINCEMEAT SAUCE - Combine
2 cups each cranberries and prepared
mincemeat, 3/4 c. sugar, 1/2 c. slivered almonds,
1 t. orange peel and 1/2 c. orange juice.
Cook and stir to boiling; simmer 5-10 mins
Cover and refrigerate in jars. (3 cups)

In 1677 the cranberry was noted as
the "choicest product of the colony."
In 1977 the cranberry culture is
being reintroduced to the people,
with the availability of this fruit
year round. It's the Berries!

CRANBERRY HAM RING
2 beaten eggs
1 1/2 c. soft bread crumbs
1/2 c. chopped onion
1/2 c. cranberry juice
Combine above and add:
1 1/2 lbs. ground ham
1 lb. ground pork
Mix well. Press into lightly
oiled 6-cup ring mold.
Bake at 350° for 1 1/2 hours.
Meanwhile, prepare sauce by combining
in a saucepan:
3 T. cornstarch — 1/2 c. orange juice
1 c. cranberry sauce — Dash cloves
Cook quickly, stirring constantly. Stir
in 1 cup cranberry juice. Boil.
Baste ham ring with sauce 2 or 3 times
during last 15 minutes. Pass remaining
sauce. Makes 8-10 servings.

163

CRAN-OR GLAZE - 1½ c. icing sugar, 2 t. cranberry juice, 1 t. grated orange rind. Combine to make a thin drizzle icing.

Cranberries are sorted and graded - not by color or size - by their bounce. Some devices provide a series, 10-30, steps. The firm berries bounce to the bottom like little rubber balls. The soft berries stay on the steps.

CRANBERRY MARMALADE

Remove peel from 1 grapefruit and 1 orange; scrape peel free of excess membrane. Cut peel into thin strips. Use large kettle. Combine peel with 2½ cups water; cook, covered, low heat, about 20 minutes. Section grapefruit and orange and chop. Combine with 3 cups fresh cranberries and add to peel. Simmer 10 minutes, stirring constantly. Stir in one 1¾-ounce package powdered fruit pectin.
Bring to boil; stir in 6½ cups sugar. Bring to rolling boil; boil hard 1 minute, stirring constantly. Remove from heat and skim foam. Let stand 15 minutes, stirring occasionally. Ladle into hot sterilized glasses. Seal. Makes 4 pts.

CRANDATE SAUCE

4 cups cranberries   - 1 cup sugar
1 " snipped dates   - ½ " lt. raisins
2 " water   - ¼ " vinegar
¼ teaspoon each gr. ginger + cinnamon

Combine ingredients in medium pan.
Bring to boil; boil rapidly, uncovered,
10 minutes. Stir occasionally. Chill.

Fifty years ago on the Cape, the
cranberry pickers ranged in age
from 6-60. They earned the same
amount- 1½¢ a quart. (Social ger-
ontologists note here that the
60 yr. old was the best picker of
all age groups!)

CRANPEACH SAUCE

2 cups cranberries - 1 cup lt. raisins
1 can (16oz) peach slices - 1 cup water
1 teaspoon each grated lemon + Orange peel
1 can (6oz) frozen orange juice, thawed
1 cup sugar

Combine fruits, peels and water. Bring
slowly to a boil; cook and stir 15 mins.
Stir in remaining ingredients; simmer
30 - 35 mins. till thick, stirring to prevent
sticking. Cool; cover and refrigerate.

Cranberry products are now big business. In 1963 Ocean Spray sales were about $23 million; in 1976 total sales were $130 million.

CRANBERRY VODKA PUNCH
(makes about 30 5-oz. servings)

3   32oz bottles cranberry cocktail
⅔   cup lemon juice - 2 cups orange
2   fifths VODKA   juice
½   cup sugar - 3½ c. carbonated
                    water, chilled

Combine all except carbonated water. Mix well and chill, adding water to punch bowl just before serving.

CRANBERRY-ORANGE COBBLER

1 can cranberry sauce — 1 t. grated orange peel
1 pkg. refrigerated orange Danish rolls ē icing
           ½ teaspoon gr. cinnamon
Combine cranberry, ¼ cup water, orange
peel and spice. Heat to boiling, then pour
into round baking dish. Top the hot layer
with rolls, flat side down.
Bake at 400° for 15 - 20 mins. or till rolls are
done. Spread tops with icing from orange-
roll package. Serve warm.

The Bluenoser and the Cape Codder
have much in common. It is observed
that they have acquired a unique
approach to life! Could it have
anything to do with their long and
close association with the
courageous crimson of the late
fall berry, with its saucy, in-
dependent tart flavour?

CRANBERRY CREAM PUDDING
1 3¾ oz INSTANT pudding mix (Vanilla) - Dash nutmeg
1¼ cups cold milk - ½ cup dairy sour cream
¼ t. ground cinnamon   - ½ cup cranberry sauce
           Flaked coconut

Combine pudding mix, milk, sour cream and
spices. Beat until well blended. Fold in the
cranberry sauce. Spoon into sherbet
glasses; chill. Garnish with coconut.

CRANBERRY MELON SALAD

1 3 oz pkg. raspberry gelatin
1 10 oz pkg. frozen mixed melon balls
¼ cup ruby port wine
1 cup ground cranberries

Dissolve gelatin as directed. Stir in melon balls, separating carefully. Stir in wine. Chill partially. Fold in berries. Turn into 1-qt. mold. Chill till firm.

Cranberries are professionally stored at 36° - 40°. If color needs greater intensity, increase temperature to 45° - 50°.

CRANBERRY CAMPBELL (molded salad)

Combine 1 (16 oz) can cranberry sauce with 2 (3 oz) packages orange gelatin. Heat and stir until almost boiling and gelatin is dissolved. Stir in undrained (8 ¾ oz.) can crushed pineapple and about 2 cups gingerale. When it no longer fizzes, pour into 5-cup mold. Chill till set. Garnish with orange and grapefruit sections.

1 pound of cranberries = 13½ servings of ¼ cup each when cooked. When served raw, 1 pound makes 6 servings of ½ cup each.

CHICKEN à là Yolande

⅓ c. flour — 1½ t. salt — ½ t. paprika — Dash. garlic salt

Combine in plastic bag. Add chicken and shake to coat.

(3 large chicken breasts, split lengthwise)

In large skillet, brown slowly in 4 T. butter. Turn once. Combine 1 can cranberry sauce and 1 cup souterne. Pour over chicken. Cover and simmer 35-45 mins. Place chicken on warm platter. Pass pan juices with chicken. 6 servings.

The wooden scoop is still used to pick those berries growing along the irrigation ditches. The tines formed a comb-like end that scooped the berries from the tangle of stems.

CRANBERRY NUT PUDDING PIE

1¼ cups Cranberries
¼ " brown sugar
¼ " chopped walnuts
1 egg

¼ cup sugar
½ " sifted flour
⅓ " butter (margarine)
Vanilla ice cream

Spread CRANBERRIES on bottom of buttered 9" pie plate. Sprinkle with br. sugar and nuts. Beat egg until thick; gradually add sugar, beating until blended. Add flour and melted butter; beat well. Pour batter over CRANBERRIES. Bake at 425° for 45 mins. Cut in wedges. Serve warm with ice cream. 6 servings.

FROZEN CRANBERRY-ORANGE SALAD

1 3¾ oz. pkg. vanilla whipped dessert mix
½ c. ginger ale - 1 c. cranberry-orange Relish
Prepare mix, but substitute ginger ale for
recommended water. Fold relish into mixture.
Pour into 8x8x2-inch pan and freeze till firm.
Cut in squares, place on lettuce and garnish
with red or green grape clusters.

The old wooden cranberry scoop was
more efficient than hand pickin', but
it was a hard job. A good picker
could harvest 100 lbs. in one hour.

JOAN and ERNIE'S DESSERT

2½ T. cornstarch
1 pkg. (10 ozs) frozen
  raspberries
2 c. cranberry-
  juice cocktail
⅓ c. blanched
  almonds, chopped
Heavy cream
½ c. sugar - 2 T. sugar

Mix cornstarch with ½ cup sugar in
saucepan. Press raspberries through
strainer and add syrup to cranberry
juice. Gradually stir into cornstarch
mixture. Cook slowly until smooth and
thickened. Pour into serving dishes and
chill. Just before serving, sprinkle with
2 T. sugar and almonds.
Serve with cream.

PEACH-PECAN CHICKEN (SALAD)

1½ c. sliced peaches   - 1 c. diced celery
3 c. cubed cooked chicken - 2 T. salad oil
½ c. mayonnaise   - 2 c. orange juice
¼ c. broken, toasted pecans - 1 T. vinegar
2 3oz pkgs. lemon gelatin - ½ t + ¼ t salt
1 can whole cranberry sauce

Set aside a few peach slices for garnish.
In large bowl combine peaches, chicken
and celery. In small bowl - mayonnaise,
salad oil, vinegar and salt. Pour over chicken.
Toss. Chill. Just before serving add nuts.
Toss again. Serve in centre of ring mold.
Garnish with peach slices.

It is about time we rethought on
the familiar saying, "as American as
apple pie." The apple is not a native
fruit; seeds were brought to the
new world by early colonists. But
the large American cranberry, Vaccinium
Macrocarpon, is native only to No.
America.

CRANBERRY RING : Boil together
   1 c. orange juice and 1 c. water.
Add gelatin and salt. Dissolve.
Stir in second cup orange juice.
Chill till partially set. Stir in
cranberry sauce. Pour into
6-cup ring mold. Chill 6-8 hours.

A wet harvest used a machine similar to an eggbeater. Two sets of reels rotate rapidly to churn up the water.

CHILI CRANBERRY FRANKS

1 can chili with beans
1 " cranberry sauce
1 T. instant minced onion
1 pound frankfurters (10)
10 buns, split and toasted
1 cup crushed corn chips

Combine chili, cranberry and onion. Heat to boiling, then simmer about 15 mins. Add franks and heat 10 mins. longer.

To serve, place franks on bun, top with chili-cranberry and sprinkle with crushed corn chips.

The wet harvest crop is brought to shore by hinging together 2×4s that corral the floating berries. It takes expertise to do this. The practice is known as rafting or booming.

CRANBERRY RUM SAUCE

Combine 2 c. cranberries, ½ c. pineapple juice, ¾ c. sugar, 1 t. shredded orange peel and ¼ t. shredded lemon peel. Boil. Simmer 10 mins. Remove and stir in ¼ c. rum, 2 T. butter, dash salt. Serve with Rice Pudding Mold or over Vanilla Ice Cream, or Waffles.

On the west coast a vacuum machine is
used to harvest the cranberries. It
has a long suction hose that reaches
underneath the vines.

CRANBERRY CUCUMBER MOLD

Slice 1 large pared cucumber into
blender. Cover and blend till pureed.
(You may want to stop blender to push
cucumber down from sides). Measure
cucumber, adding water to make
1 cup.
Dissolve 1 small lemon gelatin in
¼ cups boiling water. Stir in cucumber.
Chill till partially set. Pour into 6 molds.
Chill till firm.
Dressing: In blender combine -
  1 cup creamed cottage cheese
  4 T. sugar (some prefer 2 T.)
  4 t. lemon juice
  Add 2 T. milk - 1 T. at a time.
Cut 1 cup cranberry sauce into 6 slices.
Place cranberry slice on lettuce and
Top with cucumber mold and dressing.

In Wisconsin there are two growers
who sell vines. The runners are raked
from the bogs in late October. These
prunings are used to plant new bogs.
They are spread at density of 1500 lbs.
to 3 tons per acre and are diced in.
Runners take root in about 3 weeks
after soil reaches 60°F.

CRANBERRY CAPER

1¼ c. tea — 2 T. sugar — 1 T. orange juice
2 c. cranberry cocktail — 2 jiggers RUM
Dash cinnamon, all-spice and nutmeg.
Combine and shake well. Serves 4.

Commercial separating machines allow the
cranberries 7 chances to bounce over
4" high hurdles. Only the best berries
have bounce.

IRENE'S ICE CREAM PIE
- with cranberry sauce -

Roll to crumbs.. 40 vanilla wafers (1⅓c.)
Add . . . . ½ t. ground cinnamon
                         ¼ c. sugar
                         ¼ c. butter (softened)
Press firmly against bottom and sides of
9" pie plate or 8" square pan.
Bake at 375° for 8 minutes. Cool.
Filling:
  Heat together 1 can cranberry sauce
  and ¾ cup water, till well dissolved.
  Add 1 3oz pkg. strawberry gelatin. Stir.
  Spoon in 1½ pts. strawberry ice cream.
  Stir until melted. Chill till nearly set.
- Pour into shell and chill till set- 4 hours.
- Prepare whipped topping without vanilla.

N.S. cranberries are grown commer-
cially in Arichat, Oxford, Merigomish,
Bridgewater and Aylesford. Renewed
interest in the cranberry began
in 1966.

CHICKEN CRANBERRIE

1 envelope gelatin   — 1 T. lemon juice
1 16oz can whole cranberry sauce
1 8½ oz can crushed pineapple

o   o   o

1 envelope gelatin — 1½ c. chicken broth
1 c. mayonnaise   — 1 T. lemon juice
Pinch of salt

o   o   o

1½ c. diced cooked chicken
½ c. chopped celery
2 T. snipped parsley

Cranberry layer. Stir gelatin in ½ c. water
and stir over heat until dissolved. Combine
cranberry, undrained pineapple and
lemon juice. Add dissolved gelatin.
Mix well. Pour into 10 x 6 x 1½ - inch pan.
Chill till almost firm.
Chicken layer. Soften gelatin in broth.
Stir over low heat till dissolved. Gradually
stir into mayonnaise. Add 1 T. lemon juice,
and salt. Chill slightly. Add remaining
ingredients. Pour over cranberry layer.
Chill till firm.   Serves 6-8.

In 1677, three presents were sent to
King Charles II by the colonists. The
gifts were: 2 hogsheads of samp.
(Indian corn broken and boiled),
3000 codfish and 10 barrels of cranberries

CRANBERRY HOLIDAY FREEZE

Break up 1 can cranberry sauce. Stir in
1 T. lemon juice. Turn into 9x5x3-inch pan.
Combine: 1 3-oz cream cheese
        ¼ cup mayonnaise
        ¼ " Confectioners' sugar
Stir in: 1 teaspoon orange peel
        ½ cup chopped walnuts.
Fold in: 1 cup whipped cream.
Spread over cranberry mixture.
Freeze at least several hours.
Remove 10 mins. before serving.
Serves 6.

The cranberry harvest is often called
the "ruby of the bogs."

CRANBERRY COFFEE CAKE

1¼ cups flour   4 T. butter
½ " sugar   1 egg - sl. beaten
1½ t. baking powder   3 T. milk
¼ t. salt   1 t. vanilla

Sift together dry ingredients. Cut in
butter - coarse crumbly. Combine next
three and add to dry mixture. Mix well.
Spread in greased baking pan. Spoon over
with 1½ cups chopped CRANBERRIES.

Combine ½ cup flour, ½ cup br. sugar and
½ t. cinnamon. Cut in 4 T. butter till
resembles coarse crumbs. Sprinkle
over CRANBERRIES. Bake 45-50 mins. (350°).

HARD SAUCE

Cream together ⅓ cup butter, 1 cup sifted icing sugar, ¾ tsp. vanilla and 1 Tablespoon cream.
Chill and serve cold.

STEAMED PUDDING
(Cranberry Holiday)

½ c. molasses	2 tsp. soda
½ c. boiling water	1½ cups flour
1 tsp. baking powder	1 cup cranberries

Add soda to molasses and stir in the boiling water. Sift flour and baking powder and add the molasses mixture. Add flour to cranberries to coat them and then add them to the batter.

Grease 1 quart festive mold with tight cover. Place in steamer with a rack and steam for two hours. Serve with Hard Sauce.

CRANBERRY PEARS

Combine 1 cup yogurt, ½ can cranberry sauce and ¼ cup sugar and freeze overnight in small bowl. (Later scoop out with melon ball cutter) Drain 1- 29oz can pear halves, chilled, and place on lettuce. Fill each pear with scoops of frozen mixture. Sprinkle with cinnamon.

CRANBERRY CHOCOLATE CANDY

1½ c. cranberries — ½ c. sugar
1 6oz pkg. semi-sweet chocolate bits
1 6oz can evaporated milk
½ t. vanilla — 4 c. graham crackers
2 c. tiny marshmallows — ½c. pecans

Combine berries, sugar and ½c. water.
Bring to boil, then simmer 3 minutes.
Drain, reserving 2T. syrup. Melt
chocolate with milk. Stir till smooth.
Add vanilla. Stir in remaining ingredients,
cranberries, and reserved syrup.
Pat in well-greased 9×9×2-inch dish.
Chill to firm.

CRANBERRY LIQUEUR SAUCE

Is anything more appreciated
than a gift from your kitchen?
1 pound (4 cups) cranberries
½ cup orange-flavoured liqueur
1 cup light corn syrup
2 11oz cans mandarin oranges, drained

Combine berries, liqueur and syrup.
Bring to boil; simmer 5-10 minutes. Add
orange segments and heat about
3 minutes. Spoon into jars or gift
containers. Cover and refrigerate.
Serve with meat. (4½ cups)

CRANBERRY SAN FRANCISCO

6 whole cloves — 6 inches stick cinnamon
4 whole cardamon, shelled — ¼ c. sugar
1 cup light raisins — 2 c. port wine
1 32 oz bottle cranberry juice cocktail

Tie spices in cheesecloth in saucepan.
Add 2 c. cranberry juice, raisins + sugar.
Bring to a boil, then simmer, uncovered,
about 10 minutes. Remove spices.

Before serving add remaining cranberry
juice and wine. Heat to almost boiling.
Serve in mugs, adding a few raisins.

GRANVILLE WHIRLIBIRDS - GRILLED

Salt cavities of 2 3 pound ready-to-cook
broiler-fryer chickens. Mount on spit. Turn
on motor. Brush with cooking oil. Allow
about 2 hours without hood or 1¾ hours
with hood down.

Combine:
1 can jellied cranberry sauce - 2 T. lemon juice
¼ c. cooking oil - ¼ c. sauterne - 1 t. salt
¼ c. chicken broth - 1 t. snipped parsley
½ t. prepared mustard - ½ t. Worcestershire sauce
¼ t. dried rosemary - ¼ t. celery seed
Beat smooth, then add a dash of pepper.
Brush chickens often with glaze during
last hour of roasting.

179

Low CALORIE CRANBERRY SHERBET

Combine ½ cup sugar, ½ envelope unflavored gelatin (1½ teaspoons) and dash salt in saucepan. Stir in 1 cup low-calorie cranberry juice cocktail. Stir over medium heat till dissolved. Stir in 1 cup low-calorie cranberry juice cocktail, and 1 Table spoon lemon juice. Freeze in 9x5x3-inch pan.

Break into chunks in a chilled bowl, then beat with electric mixer till smooth. Return cranberry mixture to pan. Freeze firm. Makes 6 servings for weight watchers

Petite CRANSALADS

Whip 1 cup cream, dash
salt and 1/4 cup sugar.
Fold in 2 Tablespoons
mayonnaise. Mix well.
Fold in 1 16oz. can cranberry sauce
(chilled and diced) and 1/2 6-oz can
frozen orange juice concentrate (thawed).
Freeze till firm. Remove 10 mins. before
serving. Pretty pink salads with a festive air-

CRANBERRY POP PUNCH

2 large bottles cranberry juice cocktail
1 6 oz can lemonade concentrate, thawed
1/3 cup grenadine syrup
1 28 ounce bottle raspberry or
    strawberry carbonated drink, chilled

Combine fruit juices and grenadine.
Chill. Just before serving, carefully
stir in carbonated beverage. Serve
over ice. (Makes 12 cups)

CRANBERRY ORIENTAL

1 box (3 oz) orange gelatin — 1 T. lemon juice
1 jar cranberry-orange relish
2 T. chopped crystallized ginger
1 can water chestnuts, drained + chopped
1/2 t. celery seed — 1/4 c. mayonnaise
1/4 cup dairy sour cream
Dissolve gelatin in 1c. boiling water. Add
1/2 c. cold water and lemon juice. Chill.
Fold in next four ingredients. Use a 1-quart
mold and chill till firm. Unmold and use
with dressing of sour cream and mayonnaise.

SNOWDRIFT PIE

1¼ — cups fine graham cracker crumbs
¼ — cup sugar
6 — Tablespoons butter, melted
1 — 2- or 2⅛-oz pkg. dessert topping mix
1 — 3-oz pkg. cream cheese, soft
½ — cup sugar
1 — envelope unflavored gelatin
½ — cup cold water
1 — 16-oz can cranberry sauce
¼ — teaspoon grated orange peel

Combine crumbs, ¼ c. sugar and melted butter. Line 9" plate. Bake 6-8 mins. (375°). Cool.

Prepare topping mix using pkg. directions, beating just to soft peaks. Add cream cheese and ¼ c. of sugar. Beat to stiff peaks. Spread on sides and bottom of cooled piecrust. Chill.

Combine ¼ c. sugar and gelatin. Add ½ c. water; cook and stir over low heat. Add cranberry sauce and orange peel; cook and stir until blended. Chill till syrupy. Gently pour over cheese mixture in crust. Refrigerate at least 8 hours.

Candied cranberries add festive touch to holiday cake glaze or icing.

CRANBERRIES IN SNOW

1 19 oz pkg. yellow cake mix
1 c. cranberries — 1 c. sugar
½ c. water — 6 egg whites — ¾ c. sugar
¼ t. cream of tartar

Prepare mix and bake in 24 cupcake tins 15-20 mins at 350°. Cool. Combine 1 c. each berries and sugar with water. Bring to boil. Cook 5-8 mins. over low heat. Cool.

Beat egg whites with c. of tartar. Add ¾ c. sugar, beating constantly, until meringue is glossy and forms stiff peaks.

Place 12 cupcakes on cookie sheet and frost each with meringue. Bake 5 mins. (450°) or until lightly browned. Cool and top each one with some of the cooked, cooled cranberries.

Repeat for remaining cupcakes, or save them for another time.
Variation: Buy unfrosted cupcakes and use canned cranberry sauce.

SPICED BAKED CRANAPPLE

Desired number firm, red, tart baking
apples. (Measured ingredients for 6 apples)
1½ cups cranberry sauce - 1 t. nutmeg
1 cup brown sugar   - 1 t. cinnamon
Wash and dry fruit. From top, scoop out
core. Fill apple with mixture, topping
with small piece of butter.
Bake at 375° for 30 mins. or until soft.

CRANBERRY-ORANGE MARMALADE - with carrots

Scrape 6 carrots. Dice and cook in small
amount of water. Cook 2 cups cranberries
in water to cover. Slice 3 oranges very
thin. Add juice and grated rind of 1 lemon.
Drain berries, then combine everything.
Measure and add ⅔ᵈˢ as much sugar.
Heat and stir until sugar is dissolved.
Cook rapidly until thick and clear. Pour
into clean hot glasses. Seal with
paraffin. Makes 8 glasses.

ANNAPOLIS CONSERVE

6 oranges ⌣ 1 qt. cranberries
1 lb. raisins ⌣ 2½ c. pineapple bits
1 lb. currants ⌣ ½ lb. blanched almonds
1 c. boiling water ⌣ sugar

Peel oranges and cut into pieces. Wash
cranberries. Combine and measure.
Add an equal amount of sugar. Add fruit,
boiling water and cook rapidly until
thick. Add blanched almonds.
Pour into clean hot sterilized glasses
and seal. Makes 8 (6 oz) glasses.

CRANBERRY-QUINCE PRESERVE

3 c. cranberries	4 c. sugar
2 c. chopped apple	¼ c. orange juice
2 c. chopped quince	1 orange rind, grated

Combine in saucepan and cook slowly until thick – about 15 minutes. Stir frequently. Pack in sterilized jars and seal.
An old favorite in Nova Scotia and New England.

GRANVILLE CRANBERRY CAKE

Break up 1 can whole cranberry sauce in a buttered 8¼ x 1¾-inch pan. (I use a round ovenware cake dish). Spread evenly and dot with 2 tablespoons butter.

Prepare per directions, 1 package 1 layer size white cake mix. Pour over berries. Bake at 350° for 35-40 minutes. Stand about 10 minutes; invert on plate. Serve warm with Butter Sauce:

Cream 4 T. butter. Gradually add ½ c. sifted Confectioners' sugar, creaming until fluffy. In small saucepan, combine ½ c. cold water and 1½ t. corn starch. Cook and stir. When thick and bubbly, stir into butter mixture. Add ½ t. vinegar and 1 t. vanilla. Serve warm.

HOLIDAY MINCEMEAT PIE
- with cranberry sauce -

Combine, mix well and fill 9" two-crust piepan. - 1½ c. chopped apple
1⅓ c. sugar - 1 c. raisins
½ t. salt - ½ c. cranberry sauce
½ t. cinnamon - 1 t. grated orange peel
¼ t. cloves - ½ t. " lemon peel
¼ t. ginger - ¼ t. lemon juice

Trim edge under rim of crust. Crimp.
Cut design in top. Bake (400°) 30-35 mins.
Serve warm. Top with shredded or thin
slices of Cheddar or Sharp cheese.

CRANBERRY SPICE CAKE
½ c. butter ⌐ 1 c. sugar ⌐ 1 egg
1 c. golden raisins ⌐ ½ c. chopped nuts
1½ c. flour ⌐ ¼ t. salt ⌐ 1 t. cinnamon
1 t. each baking powder and soda
½ t. gr. cloves ⌐ ½ can cranberry sauce

Cream butter and sugar. Add egg and
beat well. Stir in raisins and nuts.
Mix dry ingredients and combine.
(Reserve ¼ c. cranberry sauce for
frosting). Stir remainder into mixture.
Spread in greased 13x9x2 inch pan
and bake in moderate oven (350°) for
40 mins. or until done. Cool in pan
on rack.
Spread with Cranberry Cheese Frosting.
(see page 78)

SANDWICH FOR SANTA

Don't buy Santa a Christmas present.
Leave him a Christmas cranberry
sandwich, and hot chocolate.
Cut 2 thin slices of homemade bread.
Spread with thin layer of butter. Put
cranberry jelly in between the slices.

Santa told
me that he
likes bananas
sliced on top
of the cranberry
jelly too!

Sometimes Santa
likes a cold
drink after his
trip down the
chimney. Buy a
stick of cinnamon
at the store and
place it in a tall
glass of bright
red cranberry
juice.
Sweet dreams!

FROZEN YULE LOG

1 can pineapple slices	1 cup mayonnaise
1/4 cup pure honey	1/2 cup maraschino
3/4 cup CRANBERRIES	cherries
1/2 cup chopped nuts	2 cups heavy cream

Drain pineapple, keeping 1/4 cup. Combine
mayonnaise with 1/4 c. syrup, honey,
cherries, cranberries and nuts. Fold
in whipped cream.
In a 2-lb. can, alternate pineapple slices
and mayonnaise mixture. Cover with
plastic and freeze.
To unmold, run spatula around can, cut
bottom from can, wrap in warm wet
towel and push to slide out.
Cover with additional nuts. Keep in
freezer until ready to serve. Slice
with sharp knife - or electric knife.

Sometimes 2 1-pound coffee cans are
used. Keep logs frozen and use as needed.

MELON DESSERT
with Cranberry

1 cup low calorie cranberry juice
1 T. cornstarch — 1 T. flaked coconut
2 T. dry white wine
Honey dew melon balls
Cantaloupe fingers
Watermelon cubes

In saucepan, mix juice and cornstarch. Cook and stir till thickened.
Stir in wine and coconut.
Serve sauce with melon in dessert dishes. Makes 1 C. sauce.

PANCAKE BALLS with CRANBERRY SAUCE
2 c. milk — 2 c. flour — ½ t. salt
3 T. sugar — 3 eggs — cranberry sauce

Beat egg yolks and add sugar. Add milk
and sifted dry ingredients alternately.
Fold in egg whites, stiffly beaten. Place
a bit of fat in each depression of your
pan. Fill ⅔ full of batter. On top, place
small amount cranberry sauce, then a
final bit of batter over the sauce.

Cook until batter bubbles, then turn
carefully and cook on other side. Serve
with cranberry jelly or dust with
powdered sugar and serve as finger
food. Be sure to have a big pot of coffee
nearby!

BAPTIST WALDORF

1 egg — ½ cup sugar
1 Tablespoon grated orange peel
2   "   cranberry juice cocktail
½ cup whipped cream
3 "   diced apple
½ " chopped celery
½ " broken walnuts
1 " jellied cranberry sauce, cubed

Beat egg in saucepan, then add sugar,
orange peel and cranberry juice.
Cook and stir over low heat till thick.
Cool well. Fold in whipped cream. Chill.
Combine apple, celery and walnuts. Fold
in dressing. Garnish with cubes.
      Serve in lettuce cups _ For 8 people

BAPTIST BOUILLON

8 cups (2 bottles) low-calorie
     cranberry juice cocktail
8 beef bouillon cubes
   Lemon slices
Bring cubes-in-juice to boil. Serve
hot or cold. Garnish with lemon.
Serves 8.

Cranberry-Popcorn Garlands

Pop about 10 cups of corn. After it has cooled, use a fine needle and red thread, and alternate popcorn and a big firm cranberry to make whatever length garland you wish. With 10 cups of popped corn, I use about 4 cups of berries. Sometimes I vary the arrangement.

I saw a beautiful tree all adorned with strands of red cranberries. It was a festive sight and a family project.

CRANBERRY POPCORN BALLS

1⅓ cups sugar   12 cups popped corn
1 cup cranberry-apple drink
2 Tablespoons light corn syrup

Butter sides of heavy 2-quart pan. Add sugar, c-a drink and syrup. Cook to hard-ball stage. Slowly pour evenly over popped corn, stirring just to mix well. Butter hands lighty and shape firmly into balls. Cool.

To store - wrap individually in clear plastic wrap. Makes eighteen 2½" balls.

CRANBERRY-PRUNE WHIP
(from Springhill, N.S.)

1 C. cooked pitted prunes – 2 egg whites
1 can jellied cranberry sauce
1/4 C. chopped nuts – dash of salt

Force prunes and 1 cup cranberry sauce through sieve. Add salt to egg whites and beat until stiff. Then add fruit mixture, a small portion at a time (beating will increase volume of the mixture). Fold in nuts and chill. Serve with dabs of remaining sauce.   6-8 servings

CRANBERRY-BANANA TOAST
(from Winnipeg)

Toasted bread slices (one side only-broiler)
Softened butter - Jellied cranberry
Sliced bananas - Brown sugar-Cinnamon

Spread untoasted side of bread with butter, then with the cranberry. Cover with sliced bananas and sprinkle with brown sugar and a dash of cinnamon. Broil slowly until bananas are light brown and sauce bubbles.

These are quick and taste good at lunch or for a snack.

192

CRANBERRY QUICK BREAD

2 c. sifted flour — 1 c. sugar — 1 t. salt
1½ t. baking powder — ½ t. baking soda
¼ c. shortening - ¾ c. pineapple juice
1 egg, beaten - 1½ c. chopped cranberries
1 c. crushed pineapple — ½ c. chopped nuts
Sift dry ingredients, then cut in the
shortening until mixture is coarse.
Combine juice and beaten egg and add
to dry mixture. Gently fold in the
cranberries, pineapple and nuts.
Spoon into 9x5x3 greased loaf pan.
Bake 1 hour at 350° or until toothpick comes out clean.
   (from Carver, Mass.)

CRANBERRY- PEAR RELISH
(from Wisconsin)
1 lb. cranberries - 1 unpeeled lemon
4 hard pears, peeled and cored
1 C. sugar - ¼ c. honey - dash of salt
Wash the 3 fruits well and force them
through medium blade of chopper.
Stir in sugar, honey and salt. Cover
and chill. Keeps 2 weeks in refrigerator. Makes about 1 quart

CRANBERRY- APPLE CRISP
(from Cape Breton)
2 c. cranberries - 1 c. granulated sugar
3 c. chopped peeled apples - 1 c. brown sugar
1½ c. rolled oats — ½ c. butter — ½ t. salt
Cream or Vanilla Ice Cream

Combine fruit with white sugar and
turn into greased 9" piepan or 8"
sq. baking dish. Mix oats, br. sugar,
butter and salt until crumbly.
Sprinkle over fruit. Bake in 375°
oven 1 hour. Serve warm with
cream. About 6 servings.

The second edition of The
CRANBERRY CONNECTION contains
some of the recipes sent in by
readers. Not all could be fitted
in, but all are much appreciated.

194

APRICOT AUTUMN SALAD

1 16-oz jar chilled fruit salad
1 " can jelled C. sauce
    (chilled and cubed)
1 C. seedless raisins or Grapes
1 22-oz can Apricot pie filling
1 C. miniature marshmallows
½ C. chopped pecans
Drain fruit salad. Fold in all except
Add nuts just before serving. nuts.

MOOSE HUNTING.

195

CRANBERRY CHRISTMAS SOUFFLÉ

MAKES about 8 servings. Can be doubled.

1 envelope + 1 t. unflavored gelatin
2¼ c. cranberry juice — 1¼ c. sugar
1½ c. fresh or frozen cranberries
5 egg whites — 1½ c. heavy cream
2 T. Confectioners' sugar — ½ t. salt

- 1. Soften gelatin in ½ c. cranberry juice.

- 2. Wash berries, reserving 16 for step 4.
Combine with ¾ cup sugar and rest
of cranberry juice. Bring to boil.
Simmer 4 mins. Remove from heat
and add gelatin. Strain into
bowl — a large one!
Cool gelatin mixture.

- 3 Beat egg whites and salt until frothy.
Add remaining sugar, beating to soft
peak stage. Whip ¾ c. of heavy cream
until stiff. Fold meringue into cream.

- 4. Pour mixture above (#3) over cranberry
mixture and gently fold in until no
trace of white remains. Chop the
reserved 16 berries and fold in.
Pour into a 6-cup soufflé dish with
high collar of wax paper. Chill
about 4 hours.

- 5. Whip remaining cream with sugar
and make rosettes on top of soufflé.
Place a cranberry in centre of
each as a variation.

FRESH - CRANBERRY CHUTNEY

1¾ c. each sugar + water
1 pound (4 C.) fresh/frozen cranberries
1 c. golden raisins — ½ c. red-wine vinegar
1½ T. curry powder — 2 T. molasses
2 T. grated or minced fresh ginger
      or 2 t. ginger powder
1 T. Worcestershire — ½ t. hot-pepper sauce
          1 t. salt

Bring sugar and water to boil. Then
simmer 5 mins. Add cranberries; cook
about 5 mins. Stir in remaining
ingredients; simmer about 15 mins,
uncovered. Stir occasionally.
Ladle into hot sterilized jars, then
seal immediately.
Makes about 2 pints.

CRANBERRIE SAUCE
Combine 2 C. cranberries, ⅓ c. orange juice
and ¾ c. sugar. Stir constantly and
bring to boil. When sugar is dissolved
mix ¼ C. sugar and 2 t. cornstarch
and add to mixture of cranberries
and orange. Cook until sauce is
thick and bubbles about 1 minute.
Stir in 1 T. shredded orange peel.
Cool and chill before serving.

CRANBERRY-MINCE PARFAITS

1 3 or 3¼ oz Vanilla pudding mix
1 c. whipped cream
   1 c. mincemeat, chilled
   1¼ c. Cranberry - Orange
     Relish.

Prepare pudding by directions. Chill. Beat smooth. Fold in whipped cream. Use 7 or 8 chilled parfait glasses. Alternate layers of mincemeat, pudding and relish

CRANBERRY MANDARIN

1 envelope creamy French salad dressing mix.
½ teaspoon grated orange peel
8 cups torn mixed salad greens
1 11-oz can MANDARIN oranges, drained
1 8-oz can jellied cranberry sauce
  (chilled and cubed)
Prepare mix, adding orange peel; chill. Toss greens and oranges in large salad bowl. Lightly fold in cranberry cubes. Pass the French dressing. Serves 8.

SWEET POTATO BAKE

Whip together 1 can sweet potatoes (18oz), drained, 1 can crushed pineapple (8½oz), drained, 1 egg, 2 T. butter, melted and ½ t. salt, pinch of pepper and ¼ t. ground nutmeg. Swirl in ½ cup canned whole CRANBERRY SAUCE. Spoon into 8 greased ramekins. Top with 1 T. whole cranberry sauce. Bake 40 mins. (350°). Serves 8.

CRANBERRY BARS

2¼ c. flour — ¾ c. sugar — ¾ t. salt
¾ t. baking powder — ¾ c. butter
2 eggs — ⅓ c. milk — 1 t. almond ext.
1 can cranberry sauce
½ c. seedless raisins — CRAN-OR GLAZE

Heat oven to 400°. Use 15 x 10 x 1 -inch jelly roll pan.
Sift flour, sugar, baking powder and salt into a bowl. Cut butter in finely. Beat together eggs, milk and almond extract. Blend into flour mixture. Spread half of mixture evenly in jelly roll pan.
Mix cranberry sauce and raisins. Spread over dough in the pan. Drop remaining dough by very small amounts over top of cranberry. (There will be little spaces between the drops.) Bake a half hour. Cool in pan. Drizzle with CRAN-OR GLAZE while still a bit warm. Makes about 75 bars, 2x1-inch size.

CRAN-MINCE TARTS

Prepare pastry and line tins for tarts.
Combine, mix well and fill tarts:
   2 c. mincemeat — 1 T. lemon juice
   3/4 c. jellied cranberry
   1 1/2 c. diced, pared, tart apples
   1/4 t. grated lemon peel

Bake in hot oven - 400°- but watch
carefully that pastry does not burn.
Serve warm.

CRANBERRY NOG

Combine 2 cups well-chilled cranberry
juice with 2 cups chilled light cream
and 1 cup honey. Beat well.
Chill and serve over ice.

FUNDY FREEZE

(lemons, cranberries
   and nuts)
1 8 oz Yogurt (lemon)
1/2 c. Cranberry sauce
1/4 c. sugar
3 T. chopped pecans

Combine everything.
Spoon into 6 paper-
lined muffin tins.
Freeze until firm.
When ready to
serve, gently
remove baking
cups.
This is pretty, too!

CRANBERRY DATE TARTS

½ C. water — ¼ orange — 1 C. sugar
1 C. chopped dates — ½ lb. cranberries
⅓ c. chopped walnuts

1 recipe of your favorite pastry.
Combine sugar + water in saucepan.
Boil 5 mins, stirring frequently. Add
cranberries, grated orange rind
and chopped orange pulp. Cook
over medium heat until berries
stop popping. Remove from heat.
Chill.

Line medium size tart tins with
pastry. (Bettie uses a "fairly sweet
pastry made with brown sugar)
Combine dates and nuts with
cranberry sauce. Fill tart shells
½ full, arrange twisted strips of
pastry across tarts, lattice-like.

Bake at 425° for 20-25 minutes
or until nicely browned. Serve
plain or with whipped or ice
cream. Makes about 10-12 tarts.

(This came from Bettie Parker in Lower Economy, N.S.)

Suggestions
for the
Creative Cook

Get well
acquainted
with the
versatile
CRANBERRY.

TREAT YOURSELF
TO A NEW RECIPE
EVERY WEEK,
It's the BERRIES!

1. When cooking roast mutton or lamb, glaze with:
   a. - 1 can cranberry sauce — ½ c. cherry jam
        2 T. port wine. Roast 1 hour, then baste.
   b. - 1 cup plump cranberries + 1 cup Rhine wine
2. Cranberry is versatile with chicken:
   a - Add 1 can cranberry sauce to stuffing:
       1 6oz wild rice, 1 T instant minced onion,
       1 3oz can sliced mushrooms, 2 c. chicken broth
   b - Glaze chicken with:
       ½ c. lt. corn syrup — ¼ t. gr. ginger
       ¼ c. cranberry cocktail — 1 T. grated orange
   c - Brown chicken, then simmer, boil, simmer:
       2 c. cranberry juice — 1 T. cornstarch
       1 T. soy sauce — 1 T. vinegar — 1 T. sugar
       ¼ c. blanched almonds — ¾ c. raisins - salt
       ¾ c. precooked rice — 1 sliced onion
       1 green pepper, cut in rings.

3. Squash with Candied Cranberries:
   Bake squash about 30 mins.
   Fill with spices, butter and 1t. corn syrup
   Bake another 15 mins. Fill with Candied
   Cranberries. Attractive and good!

4. Swiss steak has a unique taste with
   addition of cranberry cocktail.

5. Swedish Meatballs are a hit when bread
   crumbs are soaked in cranberry juice,
   before balls are formed.

6. Two recipes were received for C. doughnuts.
   1 c. sliced cranberries was added to
   basic recipe but I've had no luck with this
   one.

   Try some variations with jams and jellies
   a. - Combine frozen raspberries with
        fresh cranberries.

   b. - Use a 30 oz can sliced peaches
        with 3 c. cranberries.

   c. - Prepare apples as for Apple Jelly.
        Add equal amount of cranberry
        juice. Add, after 5 minutes boil,
        3/4 c. sugar for each cup of juice.

   d. - The most welcome gift is one that
        is made in the kitchen.

   CRANBERRY PORT JELLY can be
   given as a special gift on many
   occasions. Combine 1¼c. cranberry
   juice with 3 c. sugar. Boil 1 minute.
   Add ½ bottle pectin. Boil 1 minute.
   Stir. Add 3/4 c. Ruby Port Wine. Boil.
   Do not use for 1 week. Pour into
   sterilized jelly jars.

   Best wishes for your Cranberry Adventure
                    Beatrice Ann Buszek

New Recipes

REFERENCES

United States Department of Agriculture Bulletins
    Cranberry Culture 1903 Bulletin 176
    Cranberry Diseases and Their Control 1920 Bulletin 1081
    Cranberry Harvesting and Handling 1924 Bulletin 1402
    Cranberry Insect Problems and Suggestions for Solving 1917
       Bulletin 860
    Establishing Cranberry Fields 1924 Bulletin 2400
    Fungus Diseases of the Cultivated Cranberry 1931 Bulletin 258
    Managing Cranberry Fields 1924 Bulletin 1401
    Spoilage of Cranberries after Harvest 1918 Bulletin 714

Massachusetts Experimental Station Bulletins
    Cleaning Cranberry Bog Ditches, a New Technique 1962 Bulletin 527
    Cranberry Growing in Massachusetts 1948 Bulletin 447
    Cranberry Varieties in North America 1958 Bulletin 513
    Design of Minimum Gallonage Sprinkler Systems for Cranberry Bogs
    1965 Bulletin 532
    Modern Cultural Practice in Cranberry Growing 1969 Pub. 39
    The Cranberry Industry 1968 Bulletin 201

Assorted
    Cape Cod Yesterdays, Jos. C. Lincoln, Little Brown & Co., 1937
    Cranberries, America's Favorite Fruit, History of Culture of the
    Cranberries, Ocean Spray Cranberries, Inc.
    Cranberry Facts & Pointers, Murray R.A. Dept. of Agriculture,
    Nova Scotia Provincial Government, Truro, N.S.
    Cranberry Growing in New Jersey 1922 Beckwith, C.S. New Jersey
    Agr. Exp. Station., New Brunswick, N.J.
    Cranberry Growing in Wisconsin 1966 Dana, M.N. & Klingbell, G.C.
    Univ. Wisc. Coll. Agr. Circ. 654
    Encyclopedia Britannica
    False Blossom, The Most Destructive Cranberry Disease 1935
    Franklin, H.J. Mass. State Coll. Ext. Leaf. 154
    Growing Cranberries 1966 (reprinted 1974) Hall, I.V. Canada Dept.
    Agr. Pub. 1282
    Medical Research Reports
    Nova Scotia Fruit Growers Assoc. Annual Reports-1874 to present
    Re-sanding of Massachusetts Cranberry Bogs 1969 Cross, C.E. and
    Demoranville, I. Univ. Mass. Coop Ext. Pub. 36
    Selection and Preparation of Land for Cranberry Culture 1914 Lewis,
    C.L. Univ. Minn. Agr. Exp. Sta. Bulletin 142
    Small Fruit Culture 1975 Shoemaker, J.S. Avi Pub. Westport, Conn.

SOURCE OF CUTTINGS

Cranberries are propagated from vines. The runners are raked from the bogs after harvest in late October as a horticultural practice. These prunings are used to plant new bogs. They are spread over the prepared ground at a density of 1500 lbs. to 3 tons per acre and are disced in. The planting is done either in the fall or early spring. Runners begin rooting in about three weeks after soil temperature reaches 60 degrees F.

The recipes in this book were hand-lettered by
Beatrice Ross Buszek at Cranberrie Cottage
in Nova Scotia.